FULL MOON STAGES

Personal Notes from
50 Years of The Living Theatre

JUDITH MALINA

THREE ROOMS PRESS

NEW YORK CITY

ACKNOWLEDGEMENTS:

Thanks to Thomas S. Walker and Dennis Li for the many hours of typing and proofreading of "The Full Moon Poem." Thanks also to Brad Burgess, Leah Bachar, Ilion Troya, Jay Dobkin, Lois Kagan Mingus, Cindy Rosenthal, Karen Malpede, George Bartenieff, and Garrick Beck.

COVER AND BOOK DESIGN:
KG Design International
www.katgeorges.com

PUBLISHED BY:
Three Rooms Press, New York, NY
www.threeroomspress.com

DISTRIBUTED BY:
PGW/Perseus
www.pgw.com

DEDICATION

The Living Theatre was most influential to me in my life as a young actor. As I laid the rugs on their stage for the nightly productions or cleaned the hallways of their Magic Box Theatre or stacked programs, I knew it was all worth it just to have the experience of seeing whatever they put on each night.

As a young teenager I stood in the back watching, night after night, miracles on stage, unbeknownst that I was witnessing something that could only be described as a revolution. I can't think of any other inspiration of freedom that comes close to representing the message of The Living Theatre and its daring and monumental effects. The reason I say these words is to articulate that their vision should somehow be the force that needs to be encouraged because it does do

DEDICATION

what so few things in our world are capable of: It enlightens. It inspires. It brings forth change and the natural evolution of the spirit.

I hope that this dear and momentous artist continues to be the beacon of generations to come. She stands for love, peace, hope, rebellion, freedom, generosity, and maybe the most elusive and charismatic virtues of them all, grace.

Love you, Judith, forever.

—*Al Pacino*

FULL MOON POEM

This book is a result of the commitment of Judith Malina, co-founder of The Living Theatre, "the most radical, uncompromising, and experimental group in American theatrical history,"[1] to writing an entry about what she was doing on every full moon for fifty years, from July 1964 through July 2014.

Her original concept of this was to call this collection of notes "Full Moon Poem." With the addition of photos throughout, we have chosen to title this version *Full Moon Stages* to better represent this edition of the work as a whole.

Judith Malina and the ethos of The Living Theatre have deeply affected the work of Three Rooms Press. We are honored to be able to present this book as a tribute to her immensely profound life.

—The Editors

---

1 Tytell, John; *The Living Theatre: Art, Exile, and Outrage*; Grove Press; 1995; p. xi

FULL MOON STAGES

FULL MOON POEM

1964

Julian Beck and Judith Malina

1964

JULY

At the Full Moon in July
we arrived in Paris and
went to an Arab Cafe.

AUGUST

At the Full Moon in August
Mark Duffy went mad in London,
and Steve was hit by a truck while
marching in the streets.

SEPTEMBER

At the Full Moon in September
we gathered in a cellar in London
and spoke for the first time of
Frankenstein.

OCTOBER

At the Full Moon in
October we were rehearsing
The Mysteries in Paris.

1964

NOVEMBER

At the Full Moon in November
we played *The Brig* in Berlin for
millions on television.

DECEMBER

At the Full Moon in December
I was in jail in Passaic, New Jersey
for contempt of court.

1965

Frankenstein; *front: Steve Ben Israel*

1965

JANUARY

At the Full Moon in January I visited
Julian in jail in Danbury, Connecticut.

FEBRUARY

At the Full Moon in February we
played *The Mysteries* in the Carré
circus in Amsterdam.

MARCH

At the Full Moon in March we played
The Brig in Turin.

APRIL

At the Full Moon in April we played
The Mysteries in Rome.

MAY

At the Full Moon in May we performed
The Brig in Naples.

JUNE

At the Full Moon in June Garry was
sick in Paris.

JULY

At the Full Moon in July we had a
Chinese dinner with Elsa Morante
in Berlin.

AUGUST

At the Full Moon in August we
completed the structure for
Frankenstein in Berlin.

1965

SEPTEMBER

At the Full Moon in September
we were rehearsing *Frankenstein*
desperately in Berlin.

OCTOBER

At the Full Moon in October we
returned from Venice to Berlin.

NOVEMBER

At the Full Moon in November we
played *The Maids* and *The Mysteries*
at the Intercontinental in Frankfurt.

DECEMBER

At the Full Moon in December we
traveled from Malmö to Göteborg.

1966

The Maids; *from left: Julian Beck, William Shari*

1966

JANUARY

At the Full Moon in January we
arrived in Bologna.

FEBRUARY

At the Full Moon in February we
played *The Mysteries* in the Palazzo
Durini in Milano twice in a day.

MARCH

At the Full Moon in March we traveled
from Catania to Siracusa where we saw
the Greek Theatre by moonlight.

APRIL

At the Full Moon in April we
celebrated the Seder in a hotel room
in Banja Luka, Yugoslavia after
performing *The Mysteries*.

MAY

At the Full Moon in May we played
The Brig in Parma.

JUNE

At the Full Moon in June we
were rehearsing *Frankenstein*
in Reggio Emilia.

JULY

At the Full Moon in July we were
returning from the Theatre of Nations
in Paris, over the Alps, back to Italy.

AUGUST

At the Full Moon in August
we opened *Frankenstein* in
Reggio Emilia.

1966

SEPTEMBER

At the Full Moon in September we
played *Frankenstein* in Berlin.

OCTOBER

At the Full Moon in October we played
The Mysteries in Venice and staged the
Lachmyian juggernauts for *Antigone*.

NOVEMBER

At the Full Moon in November we
played *The Mysteries* in Amsterdam
and rehearsed the entrance of *Antigone*
with Polyneikes.

DECEMBER

At the Full Moon in December we
played *The Mysteries* in Amsterdam
and rehearsed the faces of the people
for *Antigone*.

1967

Judith and daughter Isha Manna with Salvador Dali

1967

JANUARY

At the Full Moon in January we staged the prologue for *Antigone* in Krefeld.

FEBRUARY

At the Full Moon in February we played *Antigone* in Dinslaken.

MARCH

At the Full Moon in March we rehearsed the *Bacchus Dances* in Perugia in the freezing Palazzo.

APRIL

At the Full Moon in April Julian flew to Morocco, and we played *The Maids* at the Palazzo Durini in Milano.

MAY

At the Full Moon in May we played *Frankenstein* in Naples.

JUNE

At the Full Moon in June most of the company traveled to Rome to make a movie.

JULY

At the Full Moon in July I was in the American Hospital in Paris with Isha Manna two days old.

AUGUST

At the Full Moon in August we walked with Garry in the Latin Quarter and visited the Orangerie in Paris where we were rehearsing *Frankenstein*.

1967

SEPTEMBER

At the Full Moon in September we performed *The Mysteries* in Paris and moved from Isha's birthplace on the Rue Troyon.

OCTOBER

At the Full Moon in October we performed *Antigone* in Brussels.

NOVEMBER

At the Full Moon in November we performed Bussotti's opera *Passion According to de Sade* and quelled a riot on stage with a sit-in in Bordeaux.

DECEMBER

At the Full Moon in December we performed *Antigone* in Paris.

1968

Antigone; *Judith Malina and Julian Beck*

1968

JANUARY

At the Full Moon in January we performed *Antigone* in Lucerne and rehearsed a new staging of the messenger scene.

FEBRUARY

At the Full Moon in February we were settling into Cefalú, Sicily, preparing to rehearse *Paradise Now*.

MARCH

At the Full Moon in March we were rehearsing *Paradise Now* in Cefalú and Julian made a lecture on John Cage.

APRIL

At the Full Moon in April we celebrated the Seder in Cefalú and rehearsed the Totem Poles for *Paradise Now*.

MAY

At the Full Moon in May we visited the cathedrals of Tours and Chartres and arrived in Paris at midnight at the start of the General Strike.

JUNE

At the Full Moon in June we worked on the staging of the Rites for *Paradise Now* in the garden of the Palace of the Popes in Avignon.

JULY

At the Full Moon in July we held our first rehearsal on the stage of the Cloister of the Carmelites in Avignon and read the *Texts of the Actions*.

AUGUST

At the Full Moon in August we worked on the Actions for *Paradise Now* in the garden of Voltaire's house in Geneva.

1968

SEPTEMBER

At the Full Moon in September we were on the *MS Aurelia*, holding a meeting on concientious objectors.

OCTOBER

At the Full Moon in October we played *Frankenstein* in Brooklyn.

NOVEMBER

At the Full Moon in November we played *Paradise Now* at the Massachusetts Institute of Technology for which we were bound, and attended an anti-election rally on Boston Green.

DECEMBER

At the Full Moon in December we played *The Mysteries* at Denison State Stage College in Granville, Ohio.

1969

Paradise Now; *from left: Andrew Nadelson, Rufus Collins, Steve Ben Israel, Jim Anderson*

1969

JANUARY

At the Full Moon in January we played *The Mysteries* at Hunter College in New York City.

FEBRUARY

At the Full Moon in February we played *The Mysteries* at Hays College in Hays, Kansas.

MARCH

At the Full Moon in March we arrived in San Francisco, moved into Ferlinghetti's office and took part in the occupation of the Straight Theatre.

APRIL

At the Full Moon in April we celebrated the Seder in Mid-Atlantic on the *MS Europa*.

MAY

At the Full Moon in May we were in Grenoble worrying about a warrant for offending morals brought against *The Mysteries*, from Besançon.

MAY

At the Full Moon in May we played *Paradise Now* in St. Etienne on Julian's 44th Birthday.

JUNE

At the Full Moon in June we traveled from London to Paris en route to Morocco.

JULY

At the Full Moon in July we traveled from Essaouira to Ouarzazate at the edge of the Sahara, where Isha was sick.

AUGUST

At the Full Moon in August we were in Essaouira, finishing the text of *Paradise Now*, beginning the text of *The Mysteries*.

1969

SEPTEMBER

At the Full Moon in September we were in Taormina, rehearsing *Antigone* in the Teatro Antico and planning the new work.

OCTOBER

At the Full Moon in October I was in Paris for lunch with Jean-Jacques Lebel and took the night train to Milan where the company played *The Mysteries* in the circus.

NOVEMBER

At the Full Moon in November I was in Rome waiting for Carl to arrive, while the company played *The Mysteries* in Urbino, Italy.

DECEMBER

At the Full Moon in December we played *Paradise Now* in Bruxelles.

1970

Performing in a favela in Sao Paulo; "Christmas Cake for Hot Hole and Cold Hole;"
Mary Krapf on top of Paulo Augusto Lima, Ivan Araujo far right

1970

JANUARY

At the Full Moon in January we had an Action
Cell meeting in Pierre Clementi's house in Croissy,
planning new work.

FEBRUARY

At the Full Moon in February we
had an Action Cell meeting in Pierre
Clementi's house in Croissy, planning
new work and debating the
ideologies of revolution and violence.

MARCH

At the Full Moon in March we were still
working in Croissy making plans for
South America and a film.

APRIL

At the Full Moon in April we were still
at work in Croissy, desperate and sick
with the flu.

MAY

At the Full Moon in May we were still
working in Croissy.

JUNE

At the Full Moon in June we were still
in Croissy screaming to get out.

JULY

At the Full Moon in July we were trying
to get to Brazil, still in Paris we made a
tape about Community and shopped for
Isha's third birthday.

AUGUST

At the Full Moon in August we were
in São Paulo learning about the
Brazilian Reality.

1970

SEPTEMBER

At the Full Moon in September we were
in Rio de Janeiro working on themes,
locations and techniques for the new work.

OCTOBER

At the Full Moon in October we were in
Rio talking about making a movie and
studying Masochism.

NOVEMBER

At the Full Moon in November we were in Rio
where Lapassade and Ida talked of death, and I was
suffering and we rehearsed *Possible Rites*.

DECEMBER

At the Full Moon in December we were
in São Paulo preparing the first favela
play, taping the favela speaks.

1971

Jenny Hecht

1971

JANUARY

At the Full Moon in January we were resting in São Paulo from *Favela Play #2* on the anniversary of The Living's last performance in Berlin.

FEBRUARY

At the Full Moon in February we arrived in Montevideo and met with the Communidade del Sul.

MARCH

At the Full Moon in March we were in Ouro Preto working on the *Legacy of Cain*.

APRIL

At the Full Moon in April we celebrated a sad Seder in Ouro Preto, grieving for Jenny Hecht.

MAY

At the Full Moon in May we were rehearsing *School Project #1* with the children of the Saramenha school.

JUNE

At the Full Moon in June we were in Ouro Preto rehearsing the Direct Actions Course and the Factory play for the *Legacy of Cain.*

JULY

At the Full Moon in July we were in prison in Belo Horizonte DOPS, and Julian's mother came to take Isha out of Brazil.

AUGUST

At the Full Moon in August we were in DOPS prison in Belo Horizonte, preparing our trial.

1971

SEPTEMBER

At the Full Moon in September we arrived in New York, expulsed by the President of Brazil and met Carl Einhorn, and I made love on the roof with Abbie Hoffman.

OCTOBER

At the Full Moon in October we were in Oregon at the Rainbow family farm, with Garrick, Isha, Eden Star, making a Brazilian diorama for Yoko Ono's *Water Show*.

NOVEMBER

At the Full Moon in November we were in a motel in Oregon working on the *Enormous Despair* and the *Life of the Theatre*.

DECEMBER

At the Full Moon in December we were in San Francisco talking at the City Lights Bookstore about theatre and revolution.

1972

Judith with daughter Isha Manna

1972

JANUARY

At the Full Moon in January we were in New York City at a company meeting planning new work.

FEBRUARY

At the Full Moon in February we were on a college lecture tour traveling from Macomb University at Ann Arbor to the Rainbow People's Party.

MARCH

At the Full Moon in March we went to Harrisburg, Pennsylvania to rally at a protest of the Berrigan's imprisonment, before the Seder at Franklin's and Shirley's.

APRIL

At the Full Moon in April we were in Brooklyn working on literature and attending anti-war demonstrations.

MAY

At the Full Moon in May we went to
Philadelphia to visit Ira Einhorn.

JUNE

At the Full Moon in June we
were in Brooklyn working on the
Legacy of Cain.

JULY

At the Full Moon in July we were in Brooklyn
working on the *Legacy of Cain* and Paulo
Augusto came to visit.

AUGUST

At the Full Moon in August we flew
from San Francisco to New York.

1972

SEPTEMBER

At the Full Moon in September we were in Brooklyn working on the *Legacy of Cain*.

OCTOBER

At the Full Moon in October we attended the Paul Goodman memorial at the Unitarian Church, and went to an IWW meeting, a UCLA reception, and spent the whole night at WPLJ talking about South American prisons, and the review of *The Enormous Despair* appeared in *The New York Times*.

NOVEMBER

At the Full Moon in November we were rehearsing the *Legacy of Cain* in Brooklyn.

DECEMBER

At the Full Moon in December we demonstrated in front of Rockefeller's office on the anniversary of the Attica Massacre.

1973

1973

JANUARY

At the Full Moon in January we
rehearsed the Subway *Stop-the-War*
piece at Brooklyn Academy.

FEBRUARY

At the Full Moon in February we were
rehearsing the *Legacy of Cain* in Brooklyn.

MARCH

At the Full Moon in March we
rehearsed *The Seven Meditations* in
Brooklyn on Purim.

APRIL

At the Full Moon in April we had a Seder
with the Company in the Brooklyn house,
working on *The Tower*.

MAY

At the Full Moon in May we rehearsed
The Seven Meditations, watched Watergate
on television and celebrated Garrick's
24th birthday.

JUNE

At the Full Moon in June we made *The Tower*
chart, began building *The Tower* platforms
and went to an Anarchist meeting.

JULY

At the Full Moon in July we went to see *The
Tooth of Crime* and ate dinner with
Schechner and MacIntosh.

AUGUST

At the Full Moon in August we were
rehearsing the *Strike Support Oratorium*
in Brooklyn.

1973

SEPTEMBER

At the Full Moon in September we prepared to demonstrate against the coup in Chile, and I tripped with Reznikov.

OCTOBER

At the Full Moon in October we performed the *Chile Protest* piece on the street and I spoke at a USLA Rally at Columbia.

NOVEMBER

At the Full Moon in November we played two benefit performances of *The Seven Meditations* at the Peace Church.

DECEMBER

At the Full Moon in December we rehearsed the *Liberation Movement* at the Brooklyn Academy.

1974

At Mount Philo in Vermont; from left: Echnaton, Gypsy,
Julian Beck, Tom Walker, Judith, amd Michael Shari

1974

JANUARY

At the Full Moon in January we worked
in a Joy Cell on *The Tower* against friction
in the company.

FEBRUARY

At the Full Moon in February we worked
on the Micro Opera of Class Identification
for *The Tower* with Frederic Rzewski.

MARCH

At the Full Moon in March we protested the
garroting of a Spanish Anarchist and
rehearsed the *Farm Workers Oratorium*.

APRIL

At the Full Moon in April the police broke
up our performance of the *Oratorium* in
front of a Brooklyn Bohack's store and
we did two performances of *The Seven
Meditations* at the Peace Church.

MAY

At the Full Moon in May we gave a workshop in Amherst College in Massachusetts and performed the *Attica/Daniels Street* piece in front of the Courthouse with the students.

JUNE

At the Full Moon in June it was my forty-eighth birthday and we attended the Princeton FACT Conference and made a stir.

JULY

At the Full Moon in July we worked on *The Tower* scenario on the roof, watching the July 4th fireworks.

AUGUST

At the Full Moon in August we rehearsed *The Tower* in Mount Philo in Vermont and read *Prairie Fire* and worked on Bio-Mechanics.

1974

SEPTEMBER

At the Full Moon in September we were in
Mount Philo rehearsing *The Tower* and had
a meeting about Pittsburgh.

OCTOBER

At the Full Moon in October we
worked on the Pittsburgh Campaign
in Mount Philo.

OCTOBER

At the Full Moon in October we had a big
Halloween Party in Mount Philo.

NOVEMBER

At the Full Moon in November we were
making preparations to leave New York
for Pittsburgh.

DECEMBER

At the Full Moon in December we were
rehearsing the *Intro Play* (later *The Six Public Acts*)
in Pittsburgh.

1975

The Money Tower, Pittsburgh

1975

JANUARY

At the Full Moon in January we returned from the
Anarchist Conference in Philadelphia and worked
on *The Six Public Acts.*

FEBRUARY

At the Full Moon in February we worked
on the Cain and Abel House for *The Six
Public Acts.*

MARCH

At the Full Moon in March we met with some
Pittsburgh anarchists and worked
on texts for *The Six Public Acts.*

APRIL

At the Full Moon in April we traveled
from Cincinnati to Dayton where we
performed *The Seven Meditations.*

MAY

At the Full Moon in May we performed
Turning the Earth at a Pittsburgh Church.

JUNE

At the Full Moon in June we rehearsed
The Tower in St. Joseph's Church in
Pittsburgh.

JULY

At the Full Moon in July we rehearsed *The
Tower*'s General Strike scene in the Stephen
Foster Memorial at the University of Pittsburgh.

AUGUST

At the Full Moon in August we had
our second dress rehearsal for *The
Tower* and I designed *The Tower* money.

1975

SEPTEMBER

At the Full Moon in September we gave our last American performance of *The Tower* on the Southside in Pittsburgh.

OCTOBER

At the Full Moon in October we gave our first *Tower* performance in Venice at the Church of San Lorenzo.

NOVEMBER

At the Full Moon in November we performed *The Tower*, and Isha rehearsed for her first public *Meditations* performance in Bordeaux.

DECEMBER

At the Full Moon in December we grieved for Jim Anderson's death as we rehearsed *The Tower* and *The Meditations* and met with the Anarchs in Reggio Emilia.

1976

The Six Public Acts; *front: Julian Beck and Hanon Reznikov*

1976

JANUARY

At the Full Moon in January we performed *The Seven Meditations* in Torino and talked in the Comitato di Quartiere about plays for working people.

FEBRUARY

At the Full Moon in February we traveled from Milano to Bergamo where we worked on *Tower* rewrites and visited the Monuments of the Citta Alta.

MARCH

At the Full Moon in March we rehearsed *The Tower* in Superga.

APRIL

At the Full Moon in April we celebrated the Freedom Seder in Superga.

MAY

At the Full Moon in May we rehearsed the marching for the Occupation scene in *The Tower* and the Love House of *The Six Public Acts* in Superga.

JUNE

At the Full Moon in June we performed *The Tower* in Torino in a tent on the banks of the Po.

JULY

At the Full Moon in July we performed the *Apokatastasis* in the Piazza in Taormina to protest the reinstatement of capital punishment and we took *The Tower* set out of the Ancient Theatre by moonlight and rehearsed the *Six Public Acts* at the theatre gates.

AUGUST

At the Full Moon in August we were in Rome visiting the Pantheon, Cinècittà, Paulo Milano and Trastevere where we talk of new work, and after tears and talk prepare for Hanon's trip to America.

1976

SEPTEMBER

At the Full Moon in September we were in the
Castello Sforza in Vigevano where we learned
of the death of Mao Tse Tung.

OCTOBER

At the Full Moon in October we
performed *The Six Public Acts* to a
large crowd in the streets of Genoa.

NOVEMBER

At the Full Moon in November we
performed four of *The Six Public Acts*
in the Piazza at Faenza, and rehearsed
a feminist play.

DECEMBER

At the Full Moon in December we performed
the street play *Where Does the Violence Come
From?* in Mergillina in Napoli where the
hostile men from the MSI threw firecrackers,
and we rehearsed *The Love Play* at the Wilhelm
Reich Center and in the evening visited the
Anarchists of the Louise Michel Group.

1977

The Strike Support Oratorio; *from left: Hanon Reznikov, Steve Ben Israel, Eduardo Silva (behind)*

JANUARY

At the Full Moon in January we were in Naples doing street theatre.

FEBRUARY

At the Full Moon in February we were in Paris doing a *Love Play* workshop at Vincennes.

MARCH

At the Full Moon in March we were in Madrid, surrounded by the police for trying to play *The Seventh Meditation* in the Plaza Mayor.

APRIL

At the Full Moon in April we crossed the border between Portugal and Spain, carrying our bags of Matzohs, having celebrated a street theatre arrest in Porto, and a Seder in Coimbra.

MAY

At the Full Moon in May we were in La Chaux de Fonds preparing *The Six Public Acts* while Hanon lay healing from his operation in Lausanne.

JUNE

At the Full Moon in June we arrived in Erlangen after an all-night drive from Switzerland on Julian's 52nd birthday, and we played *The Meditations* in German in the Theatre-in-the-Garage.

JULY

At the Full Moon in July we played *The Meditations* at the Volkshaus in Zürich.

AUGUST

At the Full Moon in August we were rehearsing *Prometheus* in Rome.

1977

SEPTEMBER

At the Full Moon in September we played *The Nuclear Plague* in the Piazza Navona in Rome as part of a demonstration against nuclear power plants.

OCTOBER

At the Full Moon in October we were in Münich at a Press Conference following Julian's release from jail for defamation of the German State, and we set out for Italy, arriving at night in Bologna.

NOVEMBER

At the Full Moon in November we were rehearsing in Rome: *Prometheus* and *The Strike Support Play*.

DECEMBER

At the Full Moon in December we had a Christmas party on the day of Charlie Chaplin's death.

1978

The Love Play; *Cosenza, Italy*

1978

JANUARY

At the Full Moon in January we performed *The Meditations* at the Batschkap Theatre in Frankfurt and I wrote letters about diary publication to Kate Millet, Karen Malpede, and Bob Projansky.

FEBRUARY

At the Full Moon in February we were preparing *Prometheus* in Rome.

MARCH

At the Full Moon in March we were preparing *Prometheus* in Rome.

APRIL

At the Full Moon in April we were preparing the *Prometheus* text in Rome.

MAY

At the Full Moon in May we were rehearsing the *Prometheus* Hell Cantata in Rome.

JUNE

At the Full Moon in June we were staging the *Prometheus* Tableaux in the Teatro Alberico in Rome.

JULY

At the Full Moon in July we staged the Act I Fire Theft in *Prometheus* and gave a student workshop at the Alberico with a street performance of *The Love Play* in the Piazza San Salvatore in Lauro.

AUGUST

At the Full Moon in August we were working with Jessie Sayer on the dances for *Prometheus* in Rome.

SEPTEMBER

At the Full Moon in September we were in Prato
rehearsing the first full run through dress rehearsal of
Acts I and II of *Prometheus*.

OCTOBER

At the Full Moon in October we drove from
Liverpool to London to try to organize
performances there.

NOVEMBER

At the Full Moon in November we were
setting up the *Prometheus* set in Lille.

DECEMBER

At the Full Moon in December we played
Prometheus in Liege and vigiled under the Full
Moon in front of St. Leonard Prison.

1979

Antigone; *bottom row: Maria Nora, Tom Walker, Hanon Reznikov, Rain House; middle row: Colombe Gros-Ferray, Antonia Masulli, Catie Marchand top row: Stefan Schulberg, hidden, Christian Vollmer; top middle: Julian Beck*

JANUARY

At the Full Moon in January we performed *The Meditations* at the Sala Borromini in Rome, and after the play talked to an American ecologist and two Japanese students.

FEBRUARY

At the Full Moon in February we drove from Rome to Bologna beginning our winter tour.

MARCH

At the Full Moon in March we performed *Prometheus* in Udine at the Teatro della Mostra and vigiled at the Carcere Giudiziario.

APRIL

At the Full Moon in April I made up Hagadahs with Karen Malpede for the Seder postponed three days for the performances, and in the evening we played *Prometheus* at the Palazzino Liberty in Milano and vigiled at the San Vittore Prison.

MAY

At the Full Moon in May we were in Bologna
protesting against the review which accused
us of supporting terrorism and performed
Prometheus at the Duse Theatre.

JUNE

At the Full Moon in June we were on
the high seas on the Queen Elizabeth 2,
sailing for New York.

JULY

At the Full Moon in July we were
preparing for the London *Prometheus* at
the Roundhouse.

AUGUST

At the Full Moon in August we
traveled from Fontenay to Chalon sur
Saone, on our way back to Rome from
New York, London and Paris.

1979

SEPTEMBER

At the Full Moon in September we rehearsed the Choruses of *Antigone* in the Borghese Gardens in Rome.

OCTOBER

At the Full Moon in October Hanon and I traveled through thunderstorms from Venice to Rome, studying Greek lines, in preparation for leaving for Greece in two days.

NOVEMBER

At the Full Moon in November we met with the Greek Actors from the actors' syndicate, followed by a reception with the Mayor of Piraeus, followed by a replacement rehearsal for the actors leaving the company, and followed by a performance of *Prometheus* with an ovation.

DECEMBER

At the Full Moon in December we drove from Udine to Bergamo with Allen Ginsburg and Peter Orlovsky and Nanda Pivano and Gregory Corso, during the Poetry Reading Tour, visiting the Piazza of Udine with its lion of Venice and its Moors by noon sunlight, and the Piazza of Bergamo with its sphinxes by the Full Moon at midnight.

1980

The One and The Many; *from left: Hanon Reznikov, Judith Malina,
Christian Vollmer, Rain House, Tom Walker*

1980

JANUARY

At the Full Moon in January we were in Rome, editing diaries, poems, articles, and preparing work on a new play: Toller's *Masse-Mensch*.

FEBRUARY

At the Full Moon in February we were in Rome working on *Masse-Mensch* and we heard of the death of Romolo Valle.

MARCH

At the Full Moon in March we were in Rome, working on *Masse-Mensch* and saw Ronconi's production of Maeterlink's *Bluebird*.

MARCH

At the Full Moon in March we had our first history discussion for *Masse-Mensch* on the Eliseo Stage in Rome, and performed *Antigone* with Polyneikes with a broken foot. We postpone the Seder to its second night this Full Moon night, so that we can perform.

APRIL

At the Full Moon in April we were in Bamburg in Bavaria rehearsing the Choruses for *Masse-Mensch*, and at night took a woodland walk on Walpurgisnacht.

MAY

At the Full Moon in May we had our only dress rehearsal of *Masse-Mensch* in the tent theatre of the Free Theatre Festival on the grounds of the Olympia Park in Münich on the night before our opening.

JUNE

At the Full Moon in June we rehearsed the *House of Love* and the processions of *Six Public Acts* in the Borghese Gardens in Rome, and Isha and Eden played among the poppies, and we rehearsed the *Processions*.

JULY

At the Full Moon in July we drove from New York City to Greenfield, Massachusetts where we attended a street performance of Archibald Macleish's *Panic*, directed by Tobin and produced by Eduardo.

1980 AUGUST

At the Full Moon in August we were in Mid Atlantic on the Queen Elizabeth 2, returning to Europe, writing down the text of *Six Public Acts*, listening to the news from Poland.

SEPTEMBER

At the Full Moon in September we were in Warsaw; at the Palace of Culture and Science we saw *Man of Marble*, visited the markets, and performed *Antigone* to an ovation.

OCTOBER

At the Full Moon in October we were in Rome, rehearsing replacements for *Masse-Mensch*.

NOVEMBER

At the Full Moon in November we traveled from Rome to Asti, where we played *Antigone* at the Teatro Mago Povero.

DECEMBER

At the Full Moon in December we were in Rome at the Equinox preparing to go to New York where Mabel Beck is in the hospital.

1981

Antigone; *from left: Tom Walker, Julian Beck, Christian Vollmer*

1981

JANUARY

At the Full Moon in January we were again in Rome after a tour and a trip to New York for the death and burial of Mabel Beck, and packing to leave for a new town; we watched the inauguration of Ronald Reagan on television.

FEBRUARY

At the Full Moon in February we were in Rome rehearsing *Antigone* replacements.

MARCH

At the Full Moon in March I was in Rome again whilst the company was returning from Cento where they performed *Masse-Mensch* without me, so that I could work and rest between different towns.

APRIL

At the Full Moon in April we celebrated the Seder in an occupied house in Milano.

MAY

At the Full Moon in May we planned *Sbarcono I Turchi* for the Estate Romana at the Comune and in the Teatro of Marcello.

JUNE

At the Full Moon in June we rehearsed *Six Public Acts* in the Castello Brivio in Melegnano, for the *Together* of the Comune Baires.

JULY

At the Full Moon in July we began our first reading of *The Yellow Methuselah* in Rome.

AUGUST

At the Full Moon in August we were in Barcelona in the middle of the Spanish tour of *Masse-Mensch* and *Antigone*.

SEPTEMBER

At the Full Moon in September we traveled all day in the train from Zaragoza to Madrid, to Murcia, to Molino de Segura where we played *Antigone*, with Imke lying sick in a nearby tent. It was my thirty-eighth Wedding Anniversary.

OCTOBER

At the Full Moon in October we traveled from Rome to Paris where I studied Sonia's lines for *Masse-Mensch* in French and walked with Hanon in the Latin Quarter.

NOVEMBER

At the Full Moon in November we traveled from Lille to Paris; I was editing my 1950 diaries for Grove Press.

DECEMBER

At the Full Moon in December we were in Perpignan filming with Sheldon Rochlin and drove to Béziers where we performed *Antigone*.

1982

Judith as Lilith The Yellow Methuselah

JANUARY

At the Full Moon in January we watched the total eclipse of the Full Moon over Piazza Indipendenza during a rehearsal of *The Yellow Methuselah* in Rome.

FEBRUARY

At the Full Moon in February we went to Paris where we saw Robert Abirached who said the French government would give us 240,000 francs for *The Yellow Methuselah* and a theatre to work in, and we visited Antoine Vitez who invited us to play at the Chaillot, and Jim Haynes to plan the printing of the *Poems of a Wandering Jewess*.

MARCH

At the Full Moon in March we rehearsed the third act of *The Yellow Methuselah* at Cinecitta in Rome.

APRIL

At the Full Moon in April we celebrated the Seder in Studio 3 of the Istituto Luce in Cinecitta, after a rehearsal of the fourth act of *The Yellow Methuselah*.

MAY

At the Full Moon in May I read my poetry at Hanja's concert at the Goldoni Theatre in Rome.

JUNE

At the Full Moon in June we were in Paris planning the cover for the *Poems of a Wandering Jewess* with Jim Haynes, and having a birthday lunch with Helena and Francoise and then taking a night train to Vienna.

JULY

At the Full Moon in July we performed *Masse-Mensch* at the Epée de Bois at the Catoucherie in Paris, spoke on the *Pop Club* at the television and then went to La Coupole with Thierry and Elie.

AUGUST

At the Full Moon in August we were in Paris working on plans for the *Parisian Manicomio Play* for television, and in the evening went to see *Parsifal* at the Pagoda.

1982

SEPTEMBER

At the Full Moon in September we played *Masse-Mensch* at the Svenksa Theatre in Helsinki.

OCTOBER

At the Full Moon in October we had dinner at Jean Schore's with Kate Manheim and Richard Foreman, Jane Kramer, Ruth Henry, Leonard and Ann Guttman, William Klein and Elie, and talked about our memories of the Upper West Side.

NOVEMBER

At the Full Moon in November I was editing my diaries of 1947 to 1957 in Rome.

DECEMBER

At the first Full Moon in December I was editing my diaries of 1947 to 1957 in Rome.

DECEMBER

At the Blue Moon in December I was still editing my diaries of 1947 to 1957 in Rome.

1983

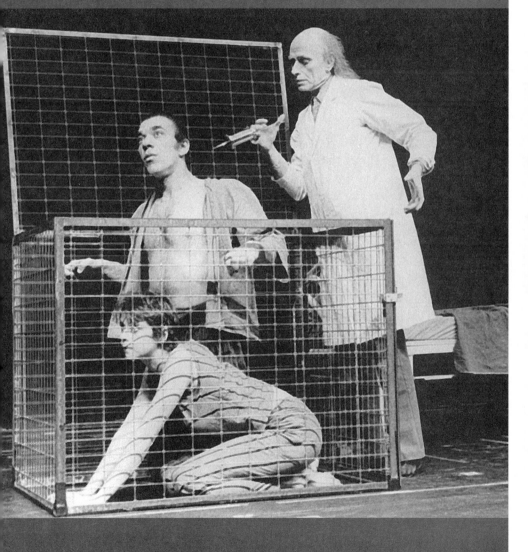

The Archaeology of Sleep; *from bottom: Maria Nora, Stefan Schulberg, Julian Beck*

1983

JANUARY

At the Full Moon in January we were packing to leave Rome amidst farewells and parties with Dario Belleza, and a $2,000 check from Grove Press for my diaries.

FEBRUARY

At the Full Moon in February we were in Tharon Plage, St. Michel Chef Chef rehearsing *The Yellow Methuselah* and preparing *The Archeology of Sleep* for Nantes.

MARCH

At the Full Moon in March we celebrated the Seder in Tharon Plage, St. Michel Chef Chef.

APRIL

At the Full Moon in April I visited Julian in the clinic, six days after his operation. He was rewriting some of *The Archeology of Sleep* scenes. I visited the doctor in the morning and learned that I too needed an operation. I rehearsed the log-rolling scene and ran through the first part of the play. Garrick consoled me through the night of my worst pains till dawn.

MAY

At the Full Moon in May we worked on *The Archeology of Sleep* in Nantes, six days before the opening, rehearsing with Isha for the role of The Sleep of Nantes, and working on the *Train of Thought*.

JUNE

At the Full Moon in June we were in Paris, recovering from surgery, and searching for a Paris theatre for The Living Theatre.

JULY

At the Full Moon in July, in Paris, we visited the Bataclan Theatre and The Rutebeuf Theatre in Clichy, while telephones rang back and forth across the Atlantic to decide whether or not Julian would play a role in Francis Ford Coppola's *Cotton Club*.

AUGUST

At the Full Moon in August I was in Paris, editing the diaries of 1958 with Hanon, and packing to join Julian in New York, filming *Cotton Club*.

1983

SEPTEMBER

At the Full Moon in September we were preparing Hanon's birthday party, and I went to his cousin Francine Tint's exhibit and walked up Fifth Avenue and saw the film *Daniel* at a War Resisters' benefit.

OCTOBER

At the Full Moon in October I was editing the final version of the 1947–1957 diaries.

NOVEMBER

At the Full Moon in November the company newly arrived in the USA met at 800 West End Ave. to make plans, and we watched together *The Day After*.

DECEMBER

At the Full Moon in December we were rehearsing *The Yellow Methuselah* in the Cuando Studios of New York; Posnick, Wilcox, Browne and Bartenieff visited.

Théâtre
hamaille
5 rue
du Ballet
NANTES
4000

1984

At the Full Moon in May, Julian, not well, visits Dr. Madden who orders
a film scan tomorrow. Garrick helps write out
invitations to my book party at Gotham Book Mart.

At the Full Moon in June Julian was in The Medical Arts Hospital,
gravely ill, where Allen Ginsberg visits him, is
gloomy and takes pictures, while Hanon calls
everywhere to find a hopeful therapy.

At the Full Moon in July Julian was in Mount Sinai Hospital
with a stomach pump and intravenous
feeding, waiting for a fever to go down to start
Chemo-Therapy.

At the Full Moon in August Julian was in Mount Sinai
recovering from a pneumonia crisis
that kept him gasping all night under
oxygen.

At the Full Moon in September Julian was at home, still very
weak, but able to take a walk on Broadway and to
receive visitors, including Ira and Timothy Baum and
Joshua Lessing who talked of giving Julian's paintings
an exhibit.

At the Full Moon in October we posed for Ron Pechette's photos and in the
evening went to The Brooklyn Academy of Music where we attended
the NY Premiere of Meredith Monk's Games, and the reception afterwards
in the Lepic Space.

At the Frosty Moon in November we attended Dario Fo's press conference at
The Joyce Theatre, and Philip Glass' Akhnaton at the City Center.

At the Full Moon in December, Julian weakened by Chemo Therapy, talks
to guests, goes downtown to a small gallery to see Beate Wheeler
and Philip Hipwells works, is recieving too-great praise for his
performance in The Cotton Club, and struggles.

Full Moon Poem in progress

1984

JANUARY

At the Full Moon in January we were taping *Antigone* which had opened and closed at the Joyce Theatre along with *The Yellow Methuselah* and *The Archeology of Sleep* and *The One and the Many*, since the last Full Moon. Then we went to Karen Malpede's and dined with Mary and Carlo and Cyrus, and Sophie, Burl, and Erika, and spoke of New York hopes.

FEBRUARY

At the Full Moon in February we taught a class at NYU, and saw Jessie dance at City Center.

MARCH

At the Full Moon in March we talked to Arthur Sainer, still saddened by the bad New York press, and Julian not feeling well.

APRIL

At the Full Moon in April Julian came out of Doctor's Hospital after surgery for a cancer recurrence, in time to celebrate the Seder with family and sixty friends, at home.

MAY

At the Full Moon in May Julian, not well, visits
Dr. Madden who orders a film scan tomorrow.
Garrick helps write out invitations to my book
party at Gotham Book Mart.

JUNE

At the Full Moon in June Julian was in the
Medical Arts Hospital, gravely ill, where
Allen Ginsberg visits him, is gloomy and takes
pictures, while Hanon calls everywhere to find a
hopeful therapy.

JULY

At the Full Moon in July Julian was in Mount
Sinai Hospital with a stomach pump and
intravenous feeding, waiting for a fever to go
down to start chemotherapy.

AUGUST

At the Full Moon in August Julian was in Mount
Sinai recovering from a pneumonia crisis that
kept him gasping all night under oxygen.

1984

SEPTEMBER

At the Full Moon in September Julian was at home, still very weak, but able to take a walk on Broadway and to receive visitors, including Ira Cohen and Timothy Baum and Joshua Lessing who talked of giving Julian's paintings an exhibit.

OCTOBER

At the Full Moon in October we posed for Ron Blanchette's photos and in the evening went to the Brooklyn Academy of Music where we attended the NY premiere of Meredith Monk's *Games*, and the reception afterward in the LePerc Space.

NOVEMBER

At the frosty moon in November we attended Dario Fo's press conference at the Joyce Theatre, and Philip Glass' *Akhnaten* at the City Center.

DECEMBER

At the Full Moon in December Julian weakened by chemotherapy, talks to guests, goes downtown to a small gallery to see Beate Wheeler and Philip Hipwell's works, is receiving too-great praise for his performance in *Cotton Club*, and struggles.

1985

Julian Beck and Judith Malina

1985

JANUARY

At the Full Moon in January Julian was rehearsing Beckett's *Lessness* with Gerald Thomas for a WBAI tape.

FEBRUARY

At the Full Moon in February we went to the Public Theatre to plan a reading and production of Michael McClure's *VKTMS*.

MARCH

At the Full Moon in March Julian and Hanon and I taught a class at New York University about The Living Theatre 14th Street, and then we watched Julian's dress rehearsal of Beckett's *That Time* at the La Mama Theatre.

APRIL

At the Full Moon in April we celebrated the Seder with our family and sixty friends; Isha read the *Mahnashtaneh*, and Baba contested the *Afikomen*; Julian read *Mammon* as is his custom, but Allen Ginsberg came just in time to read his *Holies*.

MAY

At the Full Moon in May Julian, suffering the effects of chemotherapy, read with me for Alan Alda and Martin Bregman's new movie, and in the evening we went to the Theatre for a New City to see two Rosalind Drexler plays.

JUNE

At the Full Moon in June we arrived in Frankfurt where Julian is to appear in *That Time* at the Theater Am Turm.

JULY

At the Full Moon in July Julian was working on *Theandric*, and Hanon and I were editing my 1958–1961 diaries, and we were visited by Rufus Collins with news from Amsterdam.

AUGUST

At the Full Moon in August we were back in New York, Julian taking a heavy dose of chemotherapy in preparation for the Beckett tour to Europe, while we plan The Living Theatre in New York.

1985

SEPTEMBER

At the Full Moon in September we were
in mourning for Julian who died on the
evening of the New Moon.

OCTOBER

At the Full Moon in October I participated in a
Stage Director's Panel.

NOVEMBER

At the Full Moon in November I mailed
out thanks for the participants in the Joyce
Theatre Tribute for Julian, and participated
in the Samaya Tribute.

DECEMBER

At the Full Moon in December Eden came to visit
and we opened Christmas gifts and we were sad,
Garrick, Eden, Isha, and I.

1986

Judith Malina and Hanon Reznikov

1986

JANUARY

At the Full Moon in January I was mostly grieving.

FEBRUARY

At the Full Moon in February I worked at my desk, wrote letters, had an Indian dinner with Hanon and Leah and Michael.

MARCH

At the Full Moon in March Hans Wemer Henze suggested that I direct *Stallerhof* for the Munich Festspiele. In the evening we heard a reading of Michael McClure's.

APRIL

At the Full Moon in April we taught an NYU class, and spent some time with Eden who is visiting from school.

MAY

At the Full Moon in May we read the reviews
of Julian's last film *Poltergeist II.*

JUNE

At the solstice Full Moon in June we filmed
the Hell Sequence for *Angel Heart* in New
Orleans, and under the midnight moon,
steamed up the Mississippi on the Bayou
Jean Lafitte for the wrap party.

JULY

At the Full Moon in July I spent the day with
Garrick, going through family papers, planning
the future, Isha's college, Julian's paintings.

AUGUST

At the Full Moon in August we measured
the Great Hall of the Cooper Union for
our *Retrospectacle*, speak at the Educational
Theatre Conference at NYU, deliver four
applications to the NY Foundation of the
Arts, buy Baba Israel a bat and ball as
Afikomen present, and visit Steven Ben
Israel and John Graff.

1986

SEPTEMBER

At the Full Moon in September two days after
a year without Julian, we rehearse scenes from
Desire Trapped by the Tail and *The Heroes*, for *The
Retrospectacle*, and have a "technical dinner" with
John Dodd, Bill Coco and Michael Smith.

OCTOBER

At the Full Moon in October we performed
The Living Theatre Retrospectacle in the Great
Hall of Cooper Union.

NOVEMBER

At the Full Moon in November we attended a
party at Hans Sahl's, where Rosa Von Praunheim
filmed an interview with me for a film about
Maria Piscator and Lotte Goslar.

DECEMBER

At the Full Moon in December we taught our last
NYU class of the semester ending with Artaud's
Plague and in the evening Jane Rankin
Reed and Garrick showed Julian's paintings to
John Lee from the Tibor dé Nagy Gallery.

At the Full Moon in April we were in M[...]
Passover Seder with our[...]
participants at the Teat[...]
Cultural Festiva[...]

1987

At the Full Moon [...] we were prep[...]
for a series of auditor[...]
with Karen and me, for [...]
the NYU play and for [...]
the Intrepid for Armed [...]
At the Full Moon in June I was reh[...]
in Richard II for the Sha[...]
At the Full Moon in July it was Eden[...]
and I went to hory [...]
for my performance [...]
At the Full Moon in August we were w[...]
in the evening There wer[...]
At the Full Moon in September we he[...]
dress rehearsal with spe[...]
in the Mozart Saal of the[...]
At the Full Moon in October we drove [...]
Reznick in the hospital.
At the Full Moon in November we had [...]
Malpede's US at the Tha[...]
At the Full Moon in December we were p[...]
US, and the launching [...]

1987

JANUARY

At the Full Moon in January I visited Hanon in Mount Sinai Hospital, recovering from a gall bladder operation.

FEBRUARY

At the Full Moon in February we were preparing for the collective NYU play, for *Kassandra* in Frankfurt and for the Seder in Milan, and working on Karen's *US* and on translating Hans Sahl's *Rubinstein*, while Jane Rankin Reed chooses from among Julian's drawings for the Bleecker Street exhibition.

MARCH

At the Full Moon in March I worked on the Italian *Haggadah*, though it was Purim, and worked on the stagings for the NYU play, and we attended a party at Carol Westernick's.

APRIL

At the Full Moon in April we were in Milan performing the Passover Seder with our company and one hundred spectator participants at the Teatro Pier Lombardo for the Hebrew Cultural Festival.

MAY

At the Full Moon in May we were preparing work for *Kassandra* for a series of auditions, for the Pen Women's Panel with Karen and me, for Madame Piscator's escort, for the NYU play and for a street performance at the Battleship *Intrepid* for Armed Forces Day.

JUNE

At the Full Moon in June I was rehearsing the Duchess of York in *Richard II* for the Shakespeare Festival in Central Park.

JULY

At the Full Moon in July it was Eden's sixteenth Birthday. Hanon and I went to Long Beach, and returned in time for my performance in *Richard II*.

AUGUST

At the Full Moon in August we were working on *Kassandra*, and in the evening there were visitors: Joe Chaikin, Shakti and Luke Theodore.

1987

SEPTEMBER

At the Full Moon in September we held the general probe—the final dress rehearsal with spectators—of Peter Hamel's *Kassandra* in the Mozart Saal of the Alte Oper in Frankfurt.

OCTOBER

At the Full Moon in October we drove out to Long Island to visit Hariette Reznick in hospital.

NOVEMBER

At the Full Moon in November we had the first rehearsal of Karen Malpede's *US* at the Theater for the New City.

DECEMBER

At the Full Moon in December we were preparing the production of *US,* and the launching of The Living Theatre's new campaign for its own theatre.

1988

Poster by Luba Lubova for Not In My Name!

1988

JANUARY

At the Full Moon in January we were performing *US* at the Theater for the New City, and Renfreu Neff interviewed us for *Theatre Week*, and we attended a party in honor of Hans Sahl.

FEBRURAY

At the Full Moon in February we wrote to the City's new Commissioner of Culture, Mary Campbell, for support in establishing a permanent home for The Living Theatre in NYC.

MARCH

At the Full Moon in March we taught a class at NYU on *Many Loves*, and *The Marrying Maiden*, and had a theatre business lunch with Harvey Seifter, and an Art dinner with some collectors and Ruth Escobar, our mentor, who is now a Senator in Brazil.

APRIL

At the Full Moon in April we cleaned up from the Seder, celebrated at West End Avenue, and went with Isha to see Martin Sheen and Al Pacino in *Julius Caesar* at the Public Theatre.

MAY

At the first Full Moon in May we played our final performance of *Poland/1931* at Charas.

MAY

At the Blue Moon in May we received the Silver and Bronze Medals of the University of Bologna from the Rector for our work with eighty students on *The Retrospettacolo*, visited the University's treasures and then drove to Intragna, Switzerland to begin our honeymoon.

JUNE

At the Full Moon in June I was staging my lines for Chantal Akerman's *Lost Paradise*, to school next day under the second day of the Full Moon in Williamsburg in Brooklyn.

JULY

At the Full Moon in July we rehearsed *Turning The Earth* on the campus of Columbia University, our final dress rehearsal before performances in lots and gardens.

AUGUST

At the Full Moon in August we walked on the Montauk beach in the morning, then drove from Maxine and Sheldon's back to New York, where in the evening we met with Joe Chaikin, Bill Coco and Mark Amitin to discuss *Struck Dumb*, and *War in Heaven* over Chinese dinner.

1988

SEPTEMBER

At the full moon in September we had lunch at the White Horse Tavern with Charlotte Sheedy who urged me to write a memoir and in the evening we went to see Mira Hammermesh's *Talking with the Enemy* at the Museum of Natural History.

OCTOBER

At the full moon in October we met with Crystal at the Theatre for a New City to make plans for the *VKTMS* production and I began pre-blocking.

NOVEMBER

At the Full Moon in November Wavy Gravy visited our rehearsal. A run-through of *VKTMS* in freezing cold at the Theater for the New City.

DECEMBER

At the Full Moon in December we performed *VKTMS* at the Theater for the New City; Carl Einhorn visited backstage. After which we met the Libyan Ambassador at Harold Chalmer's party, and then Mark Ernest danced naked for us at Allen Ginsberg's where we pay a sick call for his recuperation from a gall bladder operation.

1989

I and I; *Jerry Goralnick (hanging), Michael St. Claire (below) Laura Kolb (right)*

JANUARY

At the Full Moon in January we videotaped
the Shekinah scene from *Poland/1981* on
Mercer Street. At night we saw Huston's
The Dead on the VCR.

FEBRUARY

At the Full Moon in February I worked with
Beate Bennett on the translation of *I and I*.

MARCH

At the Full Moon in March a night of
screaming under the moon on Amsterdam
Avenue for *The Equalizer*, we had the first
reading of *Tablets* at 800 West End.

APRIL

At the Full Moon in April I worked with Gordon
Jacobs on the Yiddish Accent for Shifra Puah in
Enemies, a Love Story, and I worked with Erika
Bilder on the *Theandric* translation of Fanette,
and in the evening Hanon staged the Prologue
of *Tablets*.

MAY

At the Full Moon in May we were painting and plastering the walls of a new theatre on 3rd Street and Avenue C. In the evening a *Tablets* rehearsal.

JUNE

At the Full Moon in June I was sick with the flu, feverish, in bed unable to work, wrote a letter to the president of China protesting the execution of the demonstrators in Tiananmen Square.

JULY

At the Full Moon in July I was in Montreal shooting *Enemies, a Love Story* under Paul Masursky's direction.

AUGUST

At the Full Moon in August we were rehearsing *I and I* at The Living Theatre.

1989

SEPTEMBER

At the Full Moon in September I proofread the *Antigone* preface, and we were previewing *I and I*.

OCTOBER

At the Full Moon in October we were performing *I and I* at The Living Theatre, and I taught a class on Erwin Piscator at the New School with Maria Piscator and in the afternoon we met with Mel Most to discuss the Humanarchists and the IWW.

NOVEMBER

At the Full Moon in November I was working on the film *Awakenings* from 5 a.m. to 7:30 p.m., while the set was being changed from *I and I* to *Tablets* for repertory.

DECEMBER

At the Full Moon in December *Enemies, a Love Story"* just opened the night before and I had a day off from *Awakenings*, we moved furniture out of Long Beach, I had an audition for *True Colors*, and in the evening a reading at The Living Theatre with Ken Brown and Ira Cohen.

1990

THE
LIVING
THEATRE

1990

JANUARY

At the Full Moon in January we performed
I and I at The Living Theatre.

FEBRUARY

At the Full Moon in February I auditioned for a
"David Selzer Pilot" and performed *I and I*, then
celebrated Alex Kinsey's birthday.

MARCH

At the Full Moon in March we rehearsed the
German Requiem Scene 4 in the afternoon and
The Body of God in the evening.

APRIL

At the Full Moon in April we celebrated the
Seder at The Living Theatre with a hundred and
twenty people, including the homeless from *The
Body of God*.

MAY

At the Full Moon in May we opened Eric Bentley's
German Requiem with author and the press present.
My handbag is stolen after the performance.

JUNE

At the Full Moon in June I worked on the Beckett article in the morning, and on casting for *German Requiem* summer replacements, casting Charles Cragin as Sibius and then took notes on the *German Requiem* performance of the winter cast.

JULY

At the Full Moon in July we prepared to leave New York for our tour leaving tomorrow on Kuwait Airlines: A last *Tablets* rehearsal, a last company meeting, and the summer cast of *German Requiem* rehearses.

AUGUST

At the Full Moon in August we drove from Annecy to Dortmund on our way to Berlin to play *Tablets* and *I and I* in Dirk's RAMAZATA Theatre. We lunch in Geneva, passing through easy borders from Basel to Karlsruhe to Dortmund where, on Hiroshima Day and Lester's birthday, we listen to warlike news from Kuwait and Iraq.

SEPTEMBER

At the Full Moon in September we worked all day with the workshop participants creating the *Arezzo Street Play* and in the evening we had our first discussion of *The Rules of Civility* by George Washington in the mattress room at the convitto where we lodge.

OCTOBER

At the Full Moon in October we taught our NYU class *The Young Disciple* then had lunch with Karen Malpede. Hanon went to the second *Body of God* rehearsal while I went to Columbia to see my student Karl Fusari's *Camino Real*.

NOVEMBER

At the Full Moon in November we saw a possible home and theatre space on West Fourth Street. In the evening I went to the Brooklyn Academy of Music to hear Lou Harrison's *Last Symphony*, while *The Body of God* played at The Living Theatre.

DECEMBER

At the Full Moon in December I was in Hollywood to make *The Addams Family*, and saw *The Good Woman of Setzuan* while in New York HJT's *The Maids* was playing at The Living Theatre.

DECEMBER

At the Blue Moon in December we drove from Hollywood to San Diego to see in the New Year with poet and pacifist friends of the Rothenbergs and to visit Luke Theodore—for the last time.

1991

I and I; *Joanie Hieger Fritz Zosike, Philip Brehse, Victoria Murphy*

1991

JANUARY

At the Full Moon in January I was in Hollywood, on a day off from *Strenuous Mammushka* rehearsal for *The Addams Family*. I dined with Jill Taylor who gave me LA news and talked an hour with Hanon who gave me NYC News.

FEBRUARY

At the Full Moon in February I was in Hollywood shooting the Auction scene for *The Addams Family*, and at night the arrival in the car.

MARCH

At the Full Moon in March I attended a Seder in Bel Air in California at Roberta Neman's with Leo Garen while Hanon, Isha and the Company celebrated the Seder in Budapest. The first Seder of my life separate from my family.

APRIL

At the Full Moon in April we walked in Paris, visiting the Cluny, the Unicorns, the Boatman's Pillar, the old Churches and had dinner at Catie Marchand's.

MAY

At the Full Moon in May we began work on the *Waste* play, discussed Rubin's play for the Fortieth Year Benefit and attended the Mayor's annual Theatre Party at Gracie Mansion.

JUNE

At the Full Moon in June we were deep into rehearsals of the *Waste* play: preparing and rehearsing the Noh Play scene about the pollution of water.

JULY

At the Full Moon in July we opened the Waste Laboratory with installations by fifty artists and readings of poems and songs.

AUGUST

At the Full Moon in August we gave our final performance of *Waste*, on Third Street and Avenue C, outside of The Living Theatre.

SEPTEMBER

At the Full Moon in September we celebrated Hanon's forty-first birthday with a visit to Yale and in the evening Deena's workshop for the *Anarchism Play*.

OCTOBER

At the Full Moon in October we prepared the Italian tour with Fadini, and I prepared for tomorrow's appearance as Granny Addams in the Macy's Thanksgiving Day parade.

NOVEMBER

At the Full Moon in November we rehearsed the *Sixth Book* preparing for the Fortieth Anniversary Benefit. We lunched with Maria Piscator, who is sometimes angry and sometimes enthusiastic about the Piscator Seminar she is planning.

DECEMBER

At the Full Moon in December Hanon finished *The Zero Method* text and we ran through the play for the first time.

1992

Utopia; *from left: Robert Hieger, Lois Kagan-Mingus, Alan Aremius,*
Martin Reckhaus, Christian Vollmer, Gary Brackett, Marlene Lortev,
Joanie Hieger Fritz Zosike, Tom Walker (partial), Jerry Goralnick

1992

JANUARY

At the Full Moon in January we were frantically preparing for the Italian tour, and I had a last luncheon with Karen Malpede, and we dined at Dworkin and Stoltenberg's house.

FEBRUARY

At the Full Moon in February we took the ferry *Pascoli* from Naples to Palermo.

MARCH

At the Full Moon in March we were touring *The Zero Method* in the cities near Rome, and our performance in Latina was cancelled because the management didn't like us enough to advertise the play.

APRIL

At the Full Moon in April we celebrated the Seder in Brooklyn at Karen Malpede and George Bartenieff's.

MAY

At the Full Moon in May we were rehearsing
Waste, and then went to two parties,
Margaret Croydon's birthday, and Jonathan
Scheuer's.

JUNE

At the Full Moon in June we arrived in Wilmington,
North Carolina, to work on the movie *Household
Saints*, and Isha was hired to be my stand-in.

JULY

At the Full Moon in July we were in Wrightsville
Beach enjoying a few days off from a rigorous shooting
schedule, while in New York the Company prepared its
weekend performances of *Waste*.

AUGUST

At the Full Moon in August I shot my final scene
in *Household Saints*, floating, asleep like a log, in
the Blue Grotto.

1992

SEPTEMBER

At the Full Moon in September we were performing *The Zero Method* in New York City and after the show Mary gave a party for Gunter Pannewitz and many generations of Living Theatre actors gathered on *The Zero Method* set.

OCTOBER

At the Full Moon in October we were in Texas, and I worked on a staging for the first scene in *Braudel*, and in the evening we celebrated Ti and Jim's anniversary with a big party during which we watched the presidential debate.

NOVEMBER

At the Full Moon in November I worked on my Piscator notes with Jonathan Scheuer, and prepared some *Metamorphosis* notes for Maria Piscator, and Penny Arcade came to visit and we took her to an appearance on Coca Crystal's cable TV show.

DECEMBER

At the Full Moon in December I worked with John Tytell on the biography. Kathelin Hoffman came to visit from the Caravan of Dreams, and we went to a promotional party for *Household Saints* at Essex House.

1993

At the Cloître des Carmes, Avignon, France

1993

JANUARY

At the Full Moon in January Alisa Solomon interviewed us about the closing of The Third Street Theatre, and Maria Piscator wavered about her testament, and we attended Sybil Claiborne's memorial.

FEBRUARY

At the Full Moon in February we held our first *Rules of Civility* rehearsal at the Castillo Center. In the evening we saw the National Theatre of the Deaf's performance of *Ophelia* at the William Carlos Williams Center in Rutherford with Michael and Eileen Posnick.

MARCH

At the Full Moon in March we were rehearsing *The Rules of Civility* for the Theater for the New City and the German tour.

APRIL

At the Full Moon in April we celebrated The Living Theatre Seder at the home of Karen Malpede and George Bartenieff in Brooklyn.

MAY

At the Full Moon in May I was sick with the flu when I arrived in Santa Fe with Garrick. We attended a reception in the Spirit Gallery surrounded by Julian's paintings/drawings superbly framed, and then went to the home at Andrew Ungerleider and Kate Priest to stay for a few days.

JUNE

At the Full Moon in June my birthday was celebrated at the National Arts Center, with two hundred friends and promotion for *Household Saints*.

JULY

At the Full Moon in July we celebrated independence day by working on our Brazilian workshops, and visiting Lola Ross and Maria Piscator in various hospitals, and watching fireworks across the Tappan Zee in Irvington.

AUGUST

At the Full Moon in August we were in New York sending thank you notes to the Brazilians, preparing for the New Mexican tour, and visiting Maria Piscator in the psychiatric hospital.

1993

SEPTEMBER

At the Full Moon in September we were in Taos, New Mexico performing *The Rules of Civility* at the Community Auditorium, and rehearsing for the revival of *Mysteries*.

OCTOBER

At the Full Moon in October we were preparing to go into rehearsals for *Anarchia*.

NOVEMBER

At the Full Moon in November Hanon was in the hospital, his heart operation postponed at the last minute, while the Company performed his *Anarchia* monologue at Abbie Hoffman's birthday party.

DECEMBER

At the Full Moon in December Hanon was still in hospital recovering from a heart valve replacement. And I visited with Christo, the wrapper artist and friends.

1994

Not in My Name! *in Times Square*

1994

JANUARY

At the Full Moon in January we were preparing
and packing to go to California, and we visited
Mark Amitin and Maria Piscator.

FEBRUARY

At the Full Moon in February we moved from
the Rezincks in Newport Beach to an apartment
in the St. James at Hollywood and Le Brea, in the
hopes I'll find movie work.

MARCH

At the Full Moon in March we celebrated the
Seder at Karen Malpede and George Bartenieff's
house in Brooklyn.

APRIL

At the Full Moon in April I was studying *Maudie
and Jane,* and I finished the text for my Korean
speech, pre blocked the Furies/Eumenides
Scene for *Not In My Name!* and rehearsed it in
the Westbeth space.

MAY

At the Full Moon in May we traveled from New York City to Seoul, Korea for a conference and a workshop.

JUNE

At the Full Moon in June I was rehearsing *Maudie and Jane* in Asti, while Hanon went to Texas to visit his ailing father.

JULY

At the Full Moon in July we played *Maudie and Jane* outdoors in Volterra, where I saw the prisoners perform *The Brig* in the Fortress.

AUGUST

At the Full Moon in August we were rehearsing *Mysteries* in New York City, while Hanon was in Texas to be with his father.

1994

SEPTEMBER

At the Full Moon in September we were performing *Mysteries* in New York City. We visited Josie and Gizelle, and Julian's grave in Cedar Park, and went to Atlantic City.

OCTOBER

At the Full Moon in October we were in Asti, and went to the Palazzo Ottolenghi to hear Gian Luca Favetto's book presentation.

NOVEMBER

At the Full Moon in November we were in Milan rehearsing a workshop production of *A Day in the Life of the City* to to be performed in The Brera.

DECEMBER

At the Full Moon in December we were in New York City rehearsing *Not In My Name!* at the Theater for the New City.

1995

Quality of Life Crimes

1995

JANUARY

At the Full Moon in January we flew from New York to Italy to begin the next phase of the *Maudie and Jane* tour.

FEBRUARY

At the Full Moon in February we drove from the Pasolini Convegno in Pesaro to Asti and spoke at the Palazzo Ottolenghi about ensembles: The Living and the Alfieri.

MARCH

At the Full Moon in March we were in Paris for Steve Lacy's Hommage to The Living Theatre concert at the American Center, with Lacy's *Thelonies Monk Pieces* and Frederic Rzewski's *Wilde's De Profundis*, dedicated to Luke Theodore, and Hanon and I in the last scene of *Zero Method* and my songs set by Steve Lacy sung by Irene Aebi, accompanied by Rzewski and Lacy.

APRIL

At the Full Moon in April we celebrated the Seder at the cascina in Asti, with thirty people including the whole Alfieri Company, and Christina and Massimo and Claudio and Laura and their daughter Alessandra and Pietro, Candida, and Mariella Pirelli.

MAY

At the Full Moon in May we performed the workshop play *A Day in the Life of the City*, in the Palestra of Pilastro in Bologna with eighty-six participants and Antonietta Laterza. In the Evening we performed *Maudie and Jane* at the Soffitto Theatre.

JUNE

At the Full Moon in June we returned to New York City from Boston, where we participated in Tameron's secular Bar Mitzvah, called *A Rite of Passage*.

JULY

At the Full Moon in July we were in New York City attending to the exhibition of Julian's paintings, and to cardiograms, mammograms, auditions, tour bookings, and going to the theatre with friends.

AUGUST

At the Full Moon in August we flew from New York City to Milan to begin a tour of one hundred ten days and three countries, with *Living in Lautzenhausen*, *Utopia*, *The Mysteries*, and *Maudie and Jane*.

1995

SEPTEMBER

At the Full Moon in September we began blocking *Living in Lautzenhausen* in the airplane hangar in the abandoned American airbase in Hahn near the Rhine.

OCTOBER

At the Full Moon in October we saluted the full moon over the Adriatic, after rehearsing *Utopia* in Cesanatico.

NOVEMBER

At the Full Moon in November I traveled alone from Milano to Udine where I played *Maudie and Jane*, while the Living performed *Utopia* at Leoncavallo Centro Sociale in Milano. And in New York City, the Whitney Museum show *Beat Generation Culture and The New America* opened with two works by Julian Beck.

DECEMBER

At the Full Moon in December we were in San Francisco teaching a class at the American Conservatory Theatre: a twenty-five minute version of *Antigone*'s Choruses, after a morning excursion into the Redwood Forest of Miller National Park, and then for dinner with Mel Clay in his little room.

1996

Quality of Life Crimes; *from left: Johnson Anthony, Marlene Lortev, Judith Malina, Lois Kagan-Mingus, Amber, Hanon Reznikov*

1996

JANUARY

At the Full Moon in January we were rehearsing *Utopia* for its New York production at the Vineyard Theatre.

FEBRUARY

At the Full Moon in February we saw Denise Stoklos in *Un-Medea* at the La Mama, then a performance of *Utopia* in the presence of *The New York Times* with Erica Bilder as Paulina.

MARCH

At the Full Moon in March we were rehearsing *Not in My Name!* with an augmented cast of twenty-three, preparing for the next execution.

APRIL

At the Full Moon in April we performed *Not in My Name!* at NYU at an Anti-Capital Punishment Rally. Then under a total eclipse, hidden by clouds we celebrated the Seder at Karen Malpede's house with seventy people.

MAY

At the Full Moon in May I was in New York City,
writing the Commencement address for Whittier.

JUNE

At the Full Moon in June we played the *Mysteries*
in Cagliari, and rehearsed *Utopia* in Italian and got
news of the death of Timothy Leary.

JULY

At the Full Moon in July we flew from California to
New York City.

AUGUST

At the Full Moon in August we went to see the
Jewish Museum auditorium to prepare for the
winter's *Glückl*, and in the evening we performed
the protest Oratorium version of *Not in My Name!*
in Times Square for Javiar Calos Mendina.

1996

SEPTEMBER

At the Full Moon in September we were in Belgrade conducting a workshop to be performed on Sunday in the Republic Square, *A Day in the Life of Belgrade*, and in the evening attended a reception in our honor and the Open Theatre's, at the American Embassy.

OCTOBER

At the Full Moon in October Hanon and I in New York prepared his staging of Julian's *Questions* for a concert next week in Berlin with Steve Lacy and Frederic Rzewski. In the morning we went to services at Ansche Chesed, in the evening to a party at Paul McIsaacs where everyone watched the Yankees win the World Series.

NOVEMBER

At the Full Moon in November we are in New York preparing the tour for next year, working on materials for *Korach*, for other projects, and attending a reading of his memoirs by Ned Rorem at Barnes and Noble.

DECEMBER

At the Full Moon in December we paid a Christmas visit to Maria Piscator, in her one hundredth year, and we transmitted a program on the underground anarchist radio, Radio Free NY, with Penny Arcade and Al Giordano at a secret site on the Lower East Side.

1997

At the Cloitre des Carmes, Avignon, France

1997

JANUARY

At the Full Moon in January we traveled from
Milan to Foggia on our way to Lecce to play
Maudie and Jane on a seven cities tour.

FEBRUARY

At the Full Moon in February we were in New
York City giving a workshop to 20 new people
for the cast of *Not In My Name!*

MARCH

At the Full Moon in March we drove up to
Dobbs Ferry to observe the Comet Hale Bopp
on the banks of the Hudson.

APRIL

At the Full Moon in April we celebrated
the Seder at Popoli in Abruzzo, where the
Drammateatro Company serenaded us with
Yiddish songs.

MAY

At the Full Moon in May I was rehearsing *Schizophrenia* in Ljubljana, in Slovenia with the Koreodrama Theatre under Zlatar Frey's direction, dancing naked in Plečnik's Outdoor Theatre under the moon.

JUNE

At the Full Moon in June we were in Cividale del Friuli and in Udine, giving a workshop for the performance of *A Day in the Life of the City* in Udine's Piazza Libertà.

JULY

At the Full Moon in July we traveled from Varese, where we called Isha for her 30th Birthday from the Pirelli's house, to Cividale del Friuli, for a *Schizophrenia* performance.

AUGUST

At the Full Moon in August we opened *The Libation Bearers*—the Coefone—playing Clytemnestra and Aegisthes in a small Greek Amphitheatre in Palazzo-Acreid, in the ruins of the Ancient Akrai.

SEPTEMBER

At the Full Moon in September we performed *Not in My Name!* in Times Square, for a man named Mario Murphy, executed in Virginia.

OCTOBER

At the Full Moon in October we performed the *Mysteries* in Sarajevo, in the same theatre—still standing after the bombardments—where we performed it thirty-one years ago.

NOVEMBER

At the Full Moon in November I won the Rabbi Marshall T. Meyer Risk-Taker Award, at congregation B'nai Jeshurun and we performed *Not In My Name!* in the sanctuary.

DECEMBER

At the Full Moon in December we were in New York attending an underground event of Josh at the Sidewalk Cafe and had dinner with Jane Kramer at the National Arts Club who gave a talk on Allen Ginsberg, to publicize her latest work, and at a party for Eli Wallach we greeted Louise Kerz and her new husband, Al Hirshfield, and talked with Harry Belafonte who remembered the Dramatic Workshop.

1998

Judith Malina

JANUARY

At the Full Moon in January we were in Paris to present the publication of Fanette's translation of Julian's *Theandric* at the Gerard Phillipe Thêâtre, and we talk with Michelle Kokosowski about a return to Avignon this year, and we hear Grotowski talk, and we walk by the Seine.

FEBRUARY

At the Full Moon in February we were in Athens, Ohio, finishing the birthday cake of Bertolt Brecht's one-hundredth birthday celebration, and stumbled through the first ten scenes of *Mother Courage*, and I prepared for my Elizabeth Baker Evans lecture tomorrow on the events of Paris in 1968.

MARCH

At the Full Moon in March we were in Athens, Ohio working with the Athens Peace Coalition who were enthusiastic after having prevented the second Gulf War at the government's Town Meeting in Columbus, Ohio. I attended the penultimate performance of *Mother Courage* and took part in the audience discussion afterwards.

APRIL

At the Full Moon in April we celebrated the Seder at George and Karen's, with ninety people, among them Garrick and the Italians who are arranging Julian's painting exhibit for Torino, Roma, and Napoli, and I said, "Next year in our own theatre . . . "

MAY

At the Full Moon in May we went to see a lawyer about our street bust. We rehearsed *Capital Changes* at home in the evening, staging the *Mayan Pyramid in Vera Cruz* and the *Moneymen at Piacenza*.

JUNE

At the Full Moon in June we attended a memorial for Jack Frager, anarchist, at the Brecht Forum, the Pirellis return to Italy . . . and we rehearse *Capital Changes*, even on a dark night.

JULY

At the Full Moon in July we were in Spoleto for Andrea Liberovici and Eduardo Sanginnetti's *Macbeth Remix*, in which I read the *Voices of the Witches* on tape "fuori campo."

AUGUST

At the Full Moon in August we were in Palermo finishing a workshop in Santa Eulalia's deconsecrated church in the market quarter, the Vucceria, where the toughs throw Bombette (firecrackers) at us. In the night we went to Segesta where under the moon we saw Carlo Freni's Bellini event, beneath the glowing Greek temple.

1998

SEPTEMBER

At the Full Moon in September we participated in John Cage's eighty-sixth birthday reading at St. Marks, with Andrea Liberovici's tape of Cage reading Joyce's *Ulysses*, in Andrea's cut-up, while Hanon and I poured water as accompaniment from a narrow beaker to a wide beaker.

OCTOBER

At the Full Moon in October we were in New York City preparing for the coming tour, preparing our books and our poems and our own files, for a new move when we return in December.

NOVEMBER

At the Full Moon in November we were staying at Alvin Curran's in Genzano, to stoke the embers, working on Joseph and Valeska and Erwin Piscator, and driving into Rome for errands, and pleasure and a press conference.

DECEMBER

At the Full Moon in December we were in New York City, preparing the next steps.

1999

Judith Malina

JANUARY

At the Full Moon in January we read in the annual prose and poetry readings: Hanon and I read alternating pages of the last chapter of *Finnegan's Wake* at the Paula Cooper Gallery, and then, at St. Marks on the Bowery we join the poets, and Hanon reads *A Brief Walk* and I read *Others*.

JANUARY

At the Blue Moon in January we were in New York City conducting the second of two workshops to prepare a vivacious new cast for *Not In My Name!*

There is no full moon in February of 1999.

MARCH

At the Full Moon in March Dylan Foley made an oral history with me about the 60's and their consequence, then Jessica Loos made an oral history with me and Ira Cohen about Jack Micheline, then with Ira to the Calatta where we talk of literati.

MARCH

At the Full Moon in March we celebrated the Seder at Karen Malpede and George Bartenieff's house in Brooklyn with eighty people, among them Tameron.

APRIL

At the Full Moon in April we traveled from Genova to Alessandria where we signed the contract for Rocchetta Ligure with the men of the Provincia; Hanon traveled to Milano to meet with the comrades of the Eleuthera publishers for more copies of *Conversazione*, then to the Comune Baires to celebrate their thirtieth Anniversary, then to meet Piero Sciotto, the agent, about organizing us.

MAY

At the Full Moon in May we were in Asti, for a convegno on Woman's Body as Flesh = Meat/Carne.

JUNE

At the Full Moon in June we were in Rapalano, finishing an article on *Antigone* for Lorenzo to read at the Santarcangelo Convegno; and studying lines for *Ultimo Rogo* and *Capital Changes* and visiting the Siena Cathedral among the crowds gathering for the Palio.

JULY

At the Full Moon in July we were newly installed in the Centro Living Europa in the Palazzo Spinola in Rocchetta Ligure, and already we were rehearsing *Capital Changes* in Italian in our wooden-beamed rehearsal space.

AUGUST

At the Full Moon in August we were in Barcellona, Sicily touring with *Ultimo Rogo*, in Palermo at the Villa Lampedusa, in Marsala at the Carmelite convent.

SEPTEMBER

At the Full Moon in September we were at Rocchetta in the midst of rehearsals for the Italian revision of *Capital Changes*, called *Il Complesso Capitale*, to open next month in Pontedera.

OCTOBER

At the Full Moon in October we were in Rocchetta, planning and rehearsing for the official inauguration of the Centro Living Europa in the Palazzo Spinola on the sixth of next month.

NOVEMBER

At the Full Moon in November we were in New York City, my mouth full of pain from major surgery; my head full of plans for our next play, *Quality of Life Crimes*.

DECEMBER

At the Full Moon in December the moon of the Winter Solstice and the moon of the apogee, I underwent painful dentistry and then we played Mother Earth and Jupiter in Sylvie Deguiz' *Cosmic Legends* at the Kitchen in New York City.

2000

Rehearsal photo of Joanee Freedom and Judith Malina at Theater for the New City

JANUARY

At the Full Moon in January we watched the
Eclipse over the Ripa in Rocchetta, and then
traveled to Bologna to perform *Cain and Abel*
and Julian's *Questions* at the ARCI Convegno in
Chiesa San Lucia.

FEBRUARY

At the Full Moon in February we returned to
Rocchetta after a tour of *Maudie and Jane* in nine
cities from the toe to the Alps.

MARCH

At the Full Moon in March I played my last (?)
Maudie at the Duse in Bologna—while Hanon
wrote choruses for *Korach* in the dressing
room—then we drove into the night, back to
Rocchetta.

APRIL

At the Full Moon in April we celebrated the Seder in
the Palazzo Spinola in Rocchetta Ligure with six Living
Theatre members and the participation of the Mayor of
Rocchetta and sixteen neighbors.

MAY

At the Full Moon in May we were
preparing the *Resistance* play in
Rocchetta Ligure.

JUNE

At the Full Moon in June we were in New
York City, just back from Key West where
we attended Isha Manna's wedding to John
Appell, and prepared a workshop for new
actors in *Not In My Name!*

JULY

At the Full Moon in July our performance
of *Capital Changes* was rained out in
Levanto.

AUGUST

At the Full Moon in August we gathered in the
gorge at Pertuso for a *Meeting by the River* with
various entertainments, some friends from the
"territorio" and Marsha Levy Warren, and Diane,
visiting from New York and Boston.

SEPTEMBER

At the Full Moon in September we were in Rome rehearsing a workshop on the theme of the new resistance at the Snia Viscosa, and Hanon prepares for a small role in Scorsese's *Gangs of New York*.

OCTOBER

At the Full Moon in October we were in Rocchetta rehearsing the *Resistance* play. The full moon fell on Friday the 13th. I worked with Thomas Walker on the archive, and we listened, horrified to war news from Israel.

NOVEMBER

At the Full Moon in November we opened *Resistenza* at the Palazzo Spinola in Rocchetta Ligure, with an audience of two hundred, that included many participants in the historic events, and their daughters and sons and grandchildren.

DECEMBER

At the Full Moon in December we were in New York City talking about politics and the contested election on Harold Channer's cable TV show, and in the night attended the Full Moon Celebration in the Avenue B Garden.

2001

Not in My Name!; *Tripoli, Lebanon (June 2001)*

2001 JANUARY

At the Full Moon in January we were in New York City preparing for *Resistance* rehearsals in English.

FEBRUARY

At the Full Moon in February we were performing *Resistance* in New York City at the Chashama Theatre on 42nd Street, and sending out feelers for a space to live and work.

MARCH

At the Full Moon in March we were performing *Resistance* in New York City at the Chashama Theatre on 42nd Street to an audience that participated with vigor, and we saw a space on Fifth Street that we would be happy to make our home and the home of The Living Theatre.

APRIL

At the Full Moon in April we missed our plane to Palermo and spent the day in travel delays and then in the evening we performed *Love and Politics* with Pietro Pirelli, at the Lelis Theatre in Palermo.

MAY

At the Full Moon in May we performed *Not In My Name!* in the occupied Terra di Nessuno in Genova and then flew on to Catania to perform *Love and Politics* with Pietro Pirelli.

JUNE

At the Full Moon in June we were in Tripoli preparing fofty students from the University of Lebanon to perform *Not In My Name!* in Arabic in Tripoli and Beirut, and a play for the Khiam Prison site, in the south, called *Stop the Torture*. I celebrate my seventy-fifth birthday at Tripoli's House of Art where they made me cut the cake with a scimitar.

JULY

At the Full Moon in July we were in Rocchetta creating the G8 demonstration play, still to be titled, that Hanon calls *Resistance II*. In the evening we attend the last of the poetry festival readings at the Corte Theatre in Genova, with Ed Sanders and Diane di Prima and Ray Manzarek.

AUGUST

At the Full Moon in August we were in Rome, taking refuge from the rats in Rocchetta.

SEPTEMBER

At the Full Moon in September we visited the Synagogue at Mondovi.

OCTOBER

At the Full Moon in October we traveled to Livorno to conduct a *Mysteries* workshop with forty people, leading to a performance on Sunday the seventh, just as the United States began bombing Afghanistan.

OCTOBER

At the Full Moon in October we
returned from Urbino where there
was an *Hommage to Julian* at the big
Teatro Raffaello Sanzio.

NOVEMBER

At the Full Moon in November we meet Natalia in
Rome. Visited Hanja in the afternoon, then meet
Natalia in Campo dei Fiori under the Full Moon aback
Giordano Bruno. I chat with Gianni Manzelli while
Hanon talks business with Natalia, amidst Halloween
sword swallowers and kids in witches' hats . . .
Then we drove til 3am to Rocchetta.

NOVEMBER

At the Blue Moon in November we arrived in
Paris from New York to show our documentary
at Academie Esperimentale and to talk on the
aesthetics of resistance.

DECEMBER

At the Full Moon in December I was in New York
rehearsing Kafka's *The Castle* and preparing for
tomorrow's New York's Eve Party to usher in the last
palindromic year of our time.

2002

Resistenza; *Judith with the audience, Tom Walker (below right), Villa Valle Unite, Italy*

2002

JANUARY

At the Full Moon in January we were rehearsing *Resist!* for street performances during the *Protests Against the World Economic Forum* the coming weekend.

FEBRUARY

At the Full Moon in February we were in New York City looking at 330 East Eighth Street as a possible site for theatre and home; then drove to Danbury, Connecticut to attend the funeral of Rabbi Jerome Malina, my cousin who performed the wedding ceremony for me and Julian.

MARCH

At the Full Moon in March we were in Rocchetta, celebrating the Seder with twenty-one people, Hanon and I were the only Jews.

APRIL

At the Full Moon in April we were touring the Provincia of Alessandria with *Resistance*: seven cities in nine days: Valenza, Cantalupo, Ovada, Costa Vescovato, Aqui Terme, Serravalle, and Alessandria.

MAY

At the Full Moon in May we were in New York to do our interview with New York State Council of the Arts, staying to do three *Not In My Name!* performances, a poetry reading at the Pink Pony, spending time with Garrick at the Metropolitan's tapestry exhibit and apartment prospects, dining with Andrea and John, and with Karen and George, attending Lucas Reckhaus's Bar Mitzvah in the Avenue B garden, and attending Hanon's Yale Reunion of Class '72 . . . among many other activities.

JUNE

At the Full Moon in June we were in Rocchetta, where I was working on the Piscator book, while Hanon worked on the *Joseph* script. We went to Genova to see the Motus in *Twin Rooms* and the Alfieri in *Ginestra a Portella*, Luciano Nattino's play about the Sicilian bandit Giuliano.

JULY

At the Full Moon in July we were in Casalfiumanese conducting *A Day in the Life of the City* workshop with twenty seven people, and fell ill with an attack of temporary ischemia, my left side numb, my mouth unable and I went to the hospital in Imola.

AUGUST

At the Full Moon in August we were in Rocchetta working on the *Joseph* script and the Piscator book, and planning new plays, perhaps *Italian Sketches*, or *Wagner's Ring*.

SEPTEMBER

At the Full Moon in September we performed the workshop play, *Dubbio*, which we are touring to four towns, in the Atrium of the Palazzo Spinola, followed by a performance of the *Mysteries* in the Sala Nobile.

OCTOBER

At the Full Moon in October we were in Rocchetta having just finished a ten day run of *Resistance* in Genova at San Benedetto al Porto; and preparing for a trip to Aix-en-Provence for the Technoethics Conference, and then to New York—all in a week.

NOVEMBER

At the Full Moon in November we were in New York where we went to see a site on 49th Street between 9th and 10th Avenues, now just a pile of bricks and rubble . . . on which we have hopes to build home and theatre then to St. Mark's to hear Nina Zivancevic read her poems.

DECEMBER

At the Full Moon in December we were making plans for the 49th Street space, with Jacob Kain the architect, and preparing for our new play, perhaps on the theme of water.

2003

Maudie and Jane; *Judith and Pat Russell*

2003 JANUARY

At the Full Moon in January Isha and John were visiting us in New York. I was recovering from my dental ordeal and preparing for my medical ordeal, but all all our hopes were for the 49th Street space.

FEBRUARY

At the Full Moon in February we were thawing out from yesterday's big Anti-War demonstration with half a million people in the freezing wind. In the evening we went to hear Frederic Rzewski play the final section of his long piece *The Road* just as the blizzard arrived.

MARCH

At the Full Moon in March we returned from New York to Italy, arriving in Venice, flying to Milan, and meeting Marinella in Varese, where we viewed her exhibit of *Light and Shadow*, and then continued on to Rocchetta where we settled under the shadow of an eviction notice, and raging news about the Brink of War.

APRIL

At the Full Moon in April we celebrated the Seder in three languages in Rocchetta Ligure with sixteen celebrants including Henry Abramovitz' family of four direct from Jerusalem, and Pietro Pirelli and two of his friends, and two Rocchettini.

MAY

At the Full Moon in May we were in New York, planning
the 49th Street Theatre with Jacob Kain and Vanilla, in
preparation for signing the contract in Chaim Joseph's
office, making official and legal our possession of our
home and theatre-to-be.

JUNE

At the Full Moon in June we were in Rocchetta
rehearsing *Enigmas* a new play based on ideas and
notes left behind by Julian Beck.

JULY

At the Full Moon in July we were in Napoli performing
Love and Politics with Alvin Curran on the roof of The
Castel San Elmo, during the big exhibition of The Living
Theatre and Julian Beck, called *Labirinti dell' Imaginario*.

AUGUST

At the Full Moon in August we went up to
Roccaforte for the Campo Carlo Festival to
attend Marc Pujol's Kathakali performance, and
a Commedia dell'Arte performance, and to Aosta
to attend Pietro Pirelli's four hour concert of his
music for Abel Gance's film *La Roue*.

SEPTEMBER

At the Full Moon in September we were finishing
the *Enigmas* rehearsals in Rocchetta, for Napoli,
and preparing to go to New York City, after two
weeks in Napoli and a day in Bruxelles, and to leave
Rocchetta for a while (for forever?).

OCTOBER

At the Full Moon in October we were back in New York, in the whirl of its activities. Today to John Tytell's presentation of his memoir at the National Arts Club and then a tribute to Kenneth Koch at Columbia, yesterday a full day of events about avant garde theatre, honoring Mark Amitin, and tomorrow to participate in a documentary about MC Richards, while our hearts are towards the theatre space rising out of the ground at 49th Street.

NOVEMBER

At the Eclipse of the Full Moon in November we were in New York preparing the theatre, and at the hour of the Eclipse, we went up to the roof garden of our Base Camp to see the moon turn red while Steven Ben Israel recited Mary Shelley's monologue of the Creature's encounter with the full moon in *Frankenstein*.

DECEMBER

At the full moon in December we were in New York City preparing. In the morning Jonathan Lee comes to talk to me about Paul Goodman, whose life he's writing about, but whom he has never met. At lunch David Parrella comes and talks to us about his strife between the Social Sector and the Private Sector. In the evening Baba and Steve Israel and Dawn come to talk about programming events at the theatre.

2004

Do it now...

Stop the war!

Poster for The Mysteries; *top right: Rufus Collins and Judith*

JANUARY

At the Full Moon in January I was rehearsing for Rania Ajani's Katalog film, and we attended a book party for Alisa and Tony Kushner's *Wrestling with Zion*, at the new Jewish Community Center, where Tony Kushner promised us a new play for The Living Theatre.

FEBRUARY

At the Full Moon in February we were preparing in New York City. Vanilla brought the archive up to date, I worked with Hanon on *Enigmas*. And in the evening Alec Harrington came and told us of his desire to stage the Greeks.

MARCH

At the Full Moon in March I finished working on the directing book for *Enigmas*; and in the evening we went with Michael McClure and Amy to the Medicine Theatre, where we heard a reading of *VKTMS*.

APRIL

At the Full Moon in April we celebrated the Seder at
Be La Roe's in New York City with 85 Living Theatre
members and friends including Garrick and Robin and
many second generation Living Theatre people. A sweet
time was had by all—but I spoke of Fallujah.

MAY

At the Full Moon in May we met with Robert
Zuckeman of The New York State Council of
the Arts who advised us on funding. And in
the evening we attended the concert of Ned
Rorem's complete *Organ Works* performed
by Gregory D'Agostino on the great Aeolian-
Skinner organ at Riverside Church.

JUNE

At the Full Moon in June we visited the theatre space
preparing to open in December, though there is still three
inches of water on the playing space floor. We prepare the
Enigmas directing book. And we prepare for a party in
the public plaza of the World Wide Plaza for my seventy-
eighth birthday tomorrow.

JULY

At the Full Moon in July we were
working on the theatre plans, wrestling
with the zoning laws, and attended
the Actor's Temple service in our new
neighborhood synagogue.

JULY

At the Full Moon in July we attended the wedding of Baba Israel and Dawn Crandall at St. Marks in the Bowery, and we viewed a screening of Marco Pages' film about Ammon Hennacy: *Ammon Hennacy and Other Angelic Troublemakers* at The Catholic Worker's Maryhouse on East Third Street.

AUGUST

At the Full Moon in August New York City erupted in a great burst of street theatre protesting the Republican National Convention and celebrating a new world. The Living Theatre participated with a spectacle called *Code Orange Exaltations*, performed with twenty workshop participants in the midst of 500,000 demonstrators several times including performances in front of Madison Square Garden, and in Central Park on the Forbidden Great Lawn.

SEPTEMBER

At the Full Moon in September we were in Jerusalem, invited by the Acca Festival to speak at their Theatre Conference and did a scene from *Antigone*. We lived with the Abramovitz family and ate under the Full Moon in their Succoth. I was amazed at the Western Wall.

OCTOBER

At the Full Moon in October we were in Dusseldorf in Germany with the whole Company preparing our Street Play Workshop; Steve Israel also performed his latest work (first time in Europe) and Baba did his astonishing Sound Workshop called Beat Boxing.

NOVEMBER

At the Full moon in November we were in Caen, performing *Love and Politics* in Henonville at the huge art center, where there is a great exhibit of contemporary art, though not one of our best performances.

DECEMBER

At the Full Moon in December we were in New York impatiently awaiting a date for the opening of The Living Theatre on 49th Street.

2005

Eureka!; *from left: Judith, Brad Burgess, Kennedy Yanko*

JANUARY

At the Full Moon in January we were in NYC struggling with the law's delay . . . Working on our books—Hanon on *Third Street*, I on *Piscator*—Raina Ajani comes to invite us to work on her film *My Eyes Through Carnage* which she hopes to make in Libya.

FEBRUARY

At the Full Moon in February we were in NYC preparing for the new theatre, with Art/NY, and we visited the Clayton Paterson Art Gallery where Mary Beach's portrait of Julian Beck stared out at us.

MARCH

At the Full Moon in March it was Purim and we went to the *Orchid Show* at the New York Botanical Gardens. Aaron Kahn and Ira Murfin visited to talk of new projects.

APRIL

At the Full Moon in April we celebrated the Seder at George and Karen's, with Garrick and Robin and Amber and Elsa and Martha.

MAY

At the Full Moon in May we attended the FEVA-Federation of East Village Artists Festival, honoring the counter-culture heroes. Ginsberg, Ellen Stewart, Tuli Kupferberg and Jonas Mekas in a palatial Temple of Money on the Bowery, that used to be the Dime Savings Bank and is now called Capitale.

JUNE

At the Full Moon in June we were in Hillsdale, at Marsha Levy-Warren's house, working on *Joseph* and *Piscator*, when Richard Astor called about casting for *The Sopranos* and changed our plans.

JULY

At the Full Moon in July we were in New York's heatwave struggling with Haim Joseph and the lounges for the theatre. And writing about the influence of Piscator on The Living Theatre's *Capital Changes*, *Resistenza*, *A Dream of Water*, *Enigmas*, and *Not in My Name!*

AUGUST

At the Full Moon in August we were in New York, waiting eagerly for news of the theatre; working on the *Piscator* book, and Hanon gathering poetry on the internet for a piece about refugees for the *Volterra* event in October.

SEPTEMBER

At the Full Moon in September I was in Rutherford, New Jersey to celebrate William Carlos Williams' birthday, at an all-day event with scholars and writers and I introduced a staging of *A Dream of Love*, while Hanon attended the wedding of Anna Levy-Warren in Stockbridge, Massachusetts.

OCTOBER

At the Full Moon in October we were in Italy, traveling between La Spezia where we performed *Love and Politics* to Cascina where we talked and read poems before and after screenings of *Resist*.

NOVEMBER

At the Full Moon in November we were in New York, despairing of the 49th Street Theatre, Hanon made a bid for a site on Ludlow and Grand Street, to the agent Zipporal Wechsler, and the owner Bernard Kohn with high hopes . . . once again. And in the evening we attended a celebration of Karl Bissinger's work at Westbeth.

DECEMBER

At the Full Moon in December we were in Torino performing a five day workshop *Day in the Life of the City* on the Via Roma.

2006

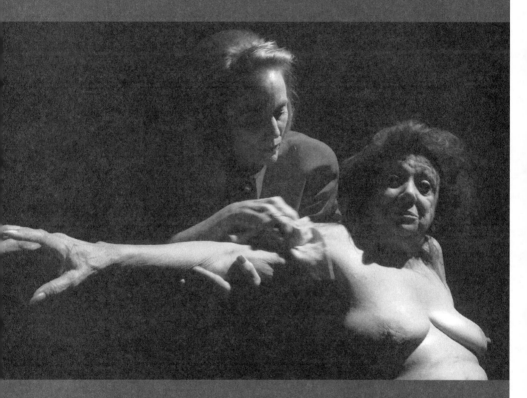

Maudie and Jane; *Pat Russell and Judith*

JANUARY

At the Full Moon in January we were
in Rome, staying at Susan and Alvin's,
preparing for our performance of *Refugee
Blues* at the Mattatoio.

FEBRUARY

At the Full Moon in February there was a blizzard in
New York and we had to cancel our performance of
Love and Politics at Makor.

MARCH

At the Full Moon in March we played the
Prince and Princess Himalay, at LaMama in
Zishan Ugurlu's production of Gombrowicz's
Operetta, followed by a performance of *Love
and Politics*, with Sylvie and Wayne, at Makor,
attended by all our friends.

APRIL

At the Full Moon in April we celebrated the Seder
at Hanon's brother's house in Newport Beach in
California, with Ti and Erik and Joyce and Andre and
with Diane and Jerome Rothenberg who read the
opening scene of *Poland 31* in Yiddish and English and
Ginsberg's *Moloch*, and on the next night still under the
Full Moon we performed *Love and Politics* in San Diego
at the Electric Lodge.

MAY

At the Full Moon in May we played *Love and Politics* in Chiasso in Switzerland, with Balbette Missoni playing Pietro Pirelli's music on the viola, while in the afternoon we conducted our *Day in the Life of the City* for the next day's performance in the Municiple Plaza.

JUNE

At the Full Moon in June we traveled from Berlin to Italy after a triumphant evening at the Akademie der Künste, showing the *Resist* film, and celebrating my eightieth birthday with our enthusiastic full house.

JULY

At the Full Moon in July we flew from New York City to Milan to begin another four week tour to include a performance of *Refugee Blues* in Torino, and getting the Palmyra Prize for Peace from Nanda Pivano in Portovenere, a five day *Mysteries* workshop in Udine, a *Love and Politics* performance at Massa at the Castello Malaspina and another at Bassano, a Poetry event in the Marble Quarries of Massa Carrara where we spoke with the anarchists of Murray Bookchin's death. A *Love and Politics* performance in Abruzzo and the Cancelli prize at Cancelli.

2006

AUGUST

At the Full Moon in August we flew from Malpensa to New York City full of plans and hopes for the new theatre.

SEPTEMBER

At the Full Moon in September Hanon went into Lenox Hill Hospital, his heart not beating in the proper rhythm, called cardiac arrhythmia, the doctors are hopeful that it isn't too serious.

OCTOBER

At the Full Moon in October we showed the Rothenbergs our Clinton Street space, with Gary Brackett, Tom Walker, Jerry Goralnick, Lois, Carlo Altomare, and Martin Reckhaus and Claire Lebowitz already there. In the evening we attended the Robert Kennedy memorial *Speak Truth to Power* with eight hundred people on Pier 60, where we greeted Janet and Martin Sheen and shook hands with President Clinton.

NOVEMBER

At the Full Moon in November we were in New York. Hanon was abed with pain, after being struck down by a motorcycle on Columbus Avenue, on the way to pick me up from trying to get an appointment for radiation therapy at Columbus hospital. I finished the Bea Arthur section of the Piscator book which is now on its way to a publisher—possibly Richard Schechner through Cindy Rosenthal. We watched the running of the New York City Marathon.

DECEMBER

At the Full Moon in December we were waiting—for the theatre to be finished— waiting for the Clinton Street apartment to be available—waiting for radiation treatments to begin—waiting to start rehearsals for *The Brig*.

2007

The Brig; *from left: Keshav Baggan, Antwan Ward, Brad Burgess, Brent Bradley, Andrew Greer, Judith, Jeff Nash, Gary Brackett, John Kohan, Morteza Tavakoli*

2007

JANUARY

At the Full Moon in January I underwent my
14th radiation treatment, and worked all day
on *The Brig* directing book, and prepared for the
visit of Eden, Keith, and Sasha tomorrow.

FEBRUARY

At the Full Moon in February I took my
twenty-seventh radiation treatment, then
rehearsed the *The Brig* with a full run-through
in the LaMama Rehearsal Studio, after which
we went to Clinton Street with Marco Nereo
Rotelli, planning the decoration of the stairwell,
then had dinner at Punch and Judy's with
Marco, Gary and Federica, who invites us to
her festival at Mantova.

MARCH

At the Full Moon in March we were rehearsing
The Brig, and Gary re-worked the set brilliantly,
lining up the ten beds symmetrically and adding
a gravel groundwork, outside the compound.
It was Purim and we heard the Megillah at the
Chosam Sofer synagogue across the street.

APRIL

At the Full Moon in April we celebrated
the Seder, the first social event in our new
theatre, with hundreds of old friends and a
beautiful ceremony.

MAY

At the Full Moon in May it was May Day
and we went to the Century Club to talk
with Horace Judson. And I had a photo
session for a *New York Times* story. In the
evening there was a musical program on
the life of Emma Goldman.

MAY

At the Full Moon in May it was Julian's birthday,
I got a Degree of Doctor of Fine Arts, in Honoris
Causa. Back at the theatre we were training
nine new maggots from a casting call, before a
performance of *The Brig*.

2007

JUNE

At the Full Moon in June I was studying my lines for the dress rehearsal of *La Guerra de Piero*, Nanda Pivano's play with texts by Fabrizio de André which opened in the Palazzo de Te in Mantova, in the presence of Fernanda Pivano. Meanwhile the rest of the company was returning to New York from Poland where they performed *The Mysteries*. And *The Brig* played in New York City making this a three cities day.

JULY

At the Full Moon in July we were in New York playing *The Brig*, and rehearsing *Maudie and Jane* and trembling with fear that the money won't hold out.

AUGUST

At the Full Moon in August we were in New York City rehearsing *Maudie and Jane*, devised from the novel *The Diary of Jane Somers* by Doris Lessing, which I've played in Italian for many years now, followed by a company meeting, at which we discussed *Eureka*.

SEPTEMBER

At the Full Moon in September we were in New York City, performing the last four *Brig* performances of a one hundred ten show run, and preparing rehearsals for *Maudie and Jane* and *Eureka*.

OCTOBER

At the Full Moon in October we were in New York City performing *The Mysteries*; and Garrick is in the city helping us to work on the archive and sales of the fancy jewelry.

NOVEMBER

At the Full Moon in November we were in Benevento, Italy, called "The City of Writers," showing the *Resist* film after performing *Love and Politics*, and I was given a prize as the great writer of contemporary theatre.

DECEMBER

At the Full Moon in December we were in New York City performing *Maudie and Jane*— the seventh performance, and celebrating the Chanukah with Tameron.

2008

The Connection; *from left: Emmanuel Harrold, Judith, John Kohan, Brad Burgess, Eno Edet*

2008

JANUARY

At the Full Moon in January I rehearsed *Maudie and Jane* with Monica Hunken as Jane to replace Pat Russel who believed she was going to China, but her engagement was cancelled on account of the huge snowstorms and Monica was cast. Pat says it's a sorrow to her. Monica improvises with each rehearsal. The Goodies, Foxy and Romy, select photos for their magazine story about me.

FEBRUARY

At the Lunar Eclipse of the Full Moon in February we performed *Maudie and Jane*, and Hanon was working with me on editing—preparing the preliminary manuscript for the *Piscator* book.

MARCH

At the Full Moon in March we slipped away to Atlantic City to escape from the pressures of the theatre, the finances, the rehearsals, and we walked on the beach and were happy.

APRIL

At the Full Moon in April we were sad at the Seder, celebrating it without Hanon who was at Beth Israel Hospital struck down by a stroke.

MAY

At the Full Moon in May we were in mourning for Hanon who died on the third of May, leaving us desolate.

JUNE

At the Full Moon in June we were struggling to keep the theatre going without Hanon and to keep ourselves from despair.

JULY

At the Full Moon in July Garrick was in New York to comfort me and to help with the organization of the theatre . . . But it's too sad.

AUGUST

At the Full Moon in August we were rehearsing *Eureka!*, working on the biomechanics of the Hydrogen Dance and the spins of the Elements.

SEPTEMBER

At the Full Moon in September we were in the midst of *Eureka!* rehearsals and began work on casting *The Connection*.

OCTOBER

At the Full Moon in October Garrick was in New York helping with the organizational-financial dilemmas of The Living Theatre. In the evening there are two events: the Anarchist Libertarian Book Club meets upstairs in the apartment and Vincent Katz's poetry reading in the theatre with thirty-one people attending and Filip Marinovich and Lewis Warsh as the readers.

NOVEMBER

At the Full Moon in November Adriana Figueirado and her daughter Marianna from Rio came to video me for her Brazilian documentary. Then I have a terrible coughing fit and panic attack. In the evening I see the Spark Plugs perform and watch Seamus McMally's film and attend Mossa Bildner's concert.

DECEMBER

At the Full Moon in December we were rehearsing *The Connection* for a New Year's Eve opening.

2009

Red/Noir; *from left: Enoch Wu, Celeste Moratti, Ondina Frate, Brent Barker*

2009

JANUARY

At the Full Moon in January we performed a matinee of *The Connection* and Alex Goldblum and I worked on foundation grants, readying a proposal for the Copani Foundation.

FEBRUARY

At the Full Moon in February we were planning the future. *The Connection* had only 5 more performances, though we are hoping to bring it back. The touring company of *The Brig* begins rehearsals with Gary Brackett and Ken Brown. I begin to work on Anne Waldman's *Red/Noir*.

MARCH

At the Full Dome Moon in March I continued to fight being sick with a heavy cough—and working on grants and *Red/Noir*, and fighting depression.

APRIL

At the Full Moon in April we celebrated the Seder in the theatre . . . with eighty people, after a trying day with police over Bambu's suicide theatre.

MAY

At the Full Moon in May we were preparing to go to Montreal's Anarchist Book Fair with a collection of scenes which is titled *The Beautiful Non Violent Anarchist Revolution Play* ending with *Marching, Free-Flow*, and *Stop the War*.

JUNE

At the Full Moon in June I was preparing the text for *Red/Noir*, and Rosa Von Praunheim did a film interview with me and two nieces of Helene Weigl.

JULY

At the Full Moon in July we watched Michael Jackson's Memorial extravagance on television, and I continued preparing *Red/Noir*.

AUGUST

At the Full Red Moon in August we went with Garrick to the Castillo where there was a screening of *Nothing Really Happens*. Then we spent the evening with Garrick making many plans.

2009

SEPTEMBER

At the Full Harvest Moon in September we attended the shiva for Marsha's father, where we met her granddaughter Amora, and where Jerry Meyer gave us $10,000 for our fundraising campaign.

OCTOBER

At the Full Dying-Grass Moon in October I finished the script for *Red/ Noir* still without casting a Glamorous Woman Detective. We meet thirty actors for the ensemble.

NOVEMBER

At the Full Frost Moon in November we were deep into *Red/Noir* rehearsals. Today Anne Waldman attended rehearsal and wrote new texts for Crystal faster than we could insert them. We rehearse the dance with Sheila and Gemma.

DECEMBER

At the Cold Full Moon in December we
had our fortieth rehearsal of *Red/Noir*, five
days before the preview at which *The New
York Times* threatens to come, and eight
days before our opening, adding lights
and films.

DECEMBER

At the Blue Moon in December we
performed *Red/Noir* to a full house,
followed by a grand New Year's Eve
Party, with Tameron and Mareba
and a theatre full of friends.

2010

Korach; *from left: Andrew Greer, Jay Dobkin, Tom Walker*

2010

JANUARY

At the Full Old Moon in January Anthony Sisco played his last performance of Jelly in *Red/Noir*, to a full house. Afterwards there was a farewell party for him that lasted until the wee hours.

FEBRUARY

At the Full Hunger Moon in February we ended the run of *Red/Noir*, after forty-four performances, with a full house and a closing party and a toast "to the next play!"

MARCH

At the Full Sugar Moon in March we celebrated the Seder in the theatre with a hundred people and Garrick and Tameron.

APRIL

At the Full Grass Moon in April I was working on *Korach* on the murmurings of the Hebrews against Moses.

MAY

At the Full Flower Moon in May it was already the second year after Hanon's death and Michael Posnick and I said a telephone's Kaddish for Hanon on the telephone together. We had been through a month of distress with the landlord, and were planing an "exit strategy" when we resolved our immediate problem with Ali, and did a benefit and performance of *Red/Noir* at the Players Club, with Isha and John present.

JUNE

At the Hot Full Moon in June I was working day and night on the *Korach* script while Brad is in misery because Yasmin told him last night that she "was seeing somebody else."

JULY

At the Full Thunder Moon in July I was sad because Garrick just left and won't be back till October, November. I worked on casting *Korach* and wrote thank you letters for three hundred dollar donations, and talked to Jay Dobkin about the role of Aaron.

AUGUST

At the Full Red Moon in August we put off further *Korach* rehearsals till September— and worked on the Axe-Houghton funding grant proposal.

SEPTEMBER

At the Full Harvest Moon in September it was Hanon's sixtieth birthday. We had just had our first *Korach* rehearsal with Carlo teaching Bio Mec. And we had some hopes for staying in our theatre, through Alan Buchman's Culture Project and a Castillo Benefit.

OCTOBER

At the Full Grass Moon in October we were rehearsing *Korach*; the trudges and the murmerings.

NOVEMBER

At the Full Beaver Moon in November we were finishing the *Korach* rehearsals, working with Carlo Altomare on the Finale, and with the new shovels. And in the evening and the night—trying to find the right poster for the film of Mahkno.

DECEMBER

At the Full Cold Moon in December it was the Solstice and a Lunar Eclipse and The Living Benefit at the Players Club.

2011

Garrick Beck and Judith in the Flamboyant Theatre at the Clemente Soto Velez Cultural Center (Jude Graham in back)

JANUARY

At the Full Old Moon in January I was fighting the winter depression. Ilion returned from Brazil and we talked about how to do the *Seven Meditations*, now that the Parrot's Perch is no longer in use. We perform *Korach* without the usual film projectors; Carlo working his Theatre Lab projector to keep the films going.

FEBRUARY

At the Full Snow Moon in February we performed the forty-first performance of *Korach*, and afterwards rehearsed the Torture Scene of *Seven Meditations on Political Sado-Masochism* with Martin Munoz and Tameron Josbeck as the Victims.

MARCH

At the Full Worm Moon in March France and the United States began bombing Libya. David Koveski interviewed me for his opera on Jimmy Spicer, and I sent my third Twitter.

APRIL

At the Full Pink Moon in April we celebrated the Seder in the front room of the apartment, since the theatre was rented out. It was a good Seder.

MAY

At the Full Flower Moon in May it was Garrick's sixty-second birthday. Brad and Tom and I traveled from Oslo in Norway to Paris in France to do workshops and workshop performances with Norwegians and Parisians.

JUNE

At the Full Rose Moon in June we finished New York rehearsals with the Motus group and Silvia Calderoni and get to work on the *History of the World.*

JULY

At the Full Hay Moon in July we were back in New York City after performing *The Plot is the Revolution* with the Motus group in Santarcangelo, working on the *History of the World.* And in the evening attended a two-and-a-half hour production of Brecht's *Life of Galileo* at Fordham University with Soraya Broukhim.

AUGUST

At the Full Green Corn Moon in August I worked all day on the mailing list while Brad's family—father, mother, sister, brother—came to take him on an excursion to Governor's Island.

2011

SEPTEMBER

At the Harvest Moon in September, we worked on preparations for the *History of the World*, and we made out a schedule for our two weekend film festival, and prepared and prepared and prepared.

OCTOBER

At the Corn-Planting Moon in October I worked on finding texts for the Piscator book, and we began rehearsals for the *History of the World*, with the audience encounter scenes.

NOVEMBER

At the Full Beaver Moon in November I was sick with my emphysema cough, nevertheless I continued pre-blocking the *History of the World*. Meanwhile Tom and Brad were in Ouro Preto rehearsing the *Brazil* play.

DECEMBER

At the Full Long Nights Moon in December we were rehearsing the *History of the World*, working on the Troubadour and on Monica Huncken's *Flying Dance* as Amelia Erhardt.

2012

Still rehearsing; Judith with Leah Bachar

2012

JANUARY

At the Full Wolf Moon in January Sylvia Calderoni and I performed *The Plot is the Revolution* at the La MaMa, Theatre with great success.

FEBRUARY

At the Full Hunger Moon in February I studied images of my hometown, Kiel, and I read my father's book *Deutsche Juden in New York*.

MARCH

At the Full Sugar Moon in March I was in New York City trying to sort out my collections and papers.

APRIL

At the Full Sprouting-Grass Moon in April we celebrated the Seder with thirtyfive people—I coughed so hard that I had to leave the Seder at meal time. Karen came up to comfort me and then went downstairs and fainted after the Seder.

MAY

At the Full Milk Moon in May I suffered from a worsening of my cough, and could barely work on assembling my final notes for the texts of the Piscator book.

JUNE

At the Full Hot Moon in June I celebrated my eighty-sixth birthday with a party that turned into a memorial event for Steven Ben Israel who died this morning.

JULY

At the Full Buck Moon in July I'm weak abed. Ilion comes to keep me company and Rene McLean drops in for half an hour to say hello. Garrick and Tameron call to say they are on their way to the Gathering.

AUGUST

At the Full Red Moon in August I wrote an afterword for my *1947–57 Diaries* for a re-publishing by Routledge. And I wrote a few sad poems about the end of life.

AUGUST

At the Blue Moon in August I was quite sick all day, coughing and choking. A little better in the evening.

2012

SEPTEMBER

At the Full Barley Moon in September we were rehearsing *Here We Are* and in the evening we celebrated the sixty-fifth anniversary of The Living Theatre at a grand dinner for forty-five people, hosted by Al Pacino at the home of Henry Jarecki.

OCTOBER

At the Full Frost Moon in October I had lunch with Garrick, as the storm clouds gathered, and in the evening the big storm Sandy broke and we were without light and electricity.

NOVEMBER

At the Full Beaver Moon in November we were rehearsing *Here We Are*—blocking out the Barcelona scene with Jay Dobkin as our friend Sam Dolgoff explaining the Spanish Anarchist Collective with bio mechanical actions that lead into the Flamenco dance.

DECEMBER

At the Full Cold Moon in December we signed the termination lease for Clinton Street. There was an interview with Claire Lebowitz. We rehearsed a run-through of *Here We Are* and then celebrated the Shabbos.

2013

At the Lillian Booth Actors Home in Englewood, New Jersey

JANUARY

At the Full Old Moon in January I sorted papers
and clothing with Leah in preparation for leaving
Clinton Street. We did the eleventh performance
of *Here We Are* without a light board man, but
got through the play well enough.

There is no entry for the Full Moon of February 2013.

MARCH

At the Full Sugar Moon in March we were
performing *Here We Are* at the Clemente Center
on the Lower East Side for four performances
after the closing of The Living Theatre on
Clinton Street, and I was living at the Lillian
Booth Actors Home in Englewood, New Jersey.

APRIL

At the Full Sprouting Grass Moon in April
I lived in Englewood at the Actor's Home,
where we projected Ali's *Love and Politics* film,
and observed the deer in the garden.

MAY

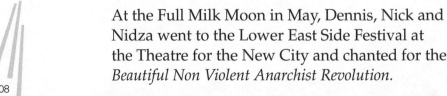

At the Full Milk Moon in May, Dennis, Nick and
Nidza went to the Lower East Side Festival at
the Theatre for the New City and chanted for the
Beautiful Non Violent Anarchist Revolution.

JUNE

At the Full Strawberry Moon in June
I was writing letters at my desk in
Englewood, desperate to get out of
New Jersey.

JULY

At the Full Thunder Moon in July Leah
and I sorted and filed the European
archive till 3:30 in the morning.

AUGUST

At the Full Red Moon in August I saw
Gone with the Wind on television.

SEPTEMBER

At the Full Barley Moon in September
I went to the hospital in Englewood,
with 102 degree fever and pneumonia.
Pierre Biner visits me there.

2013

OCTOBER

At the Full Travel Moon in October
we celebrated the Shabbos with
Joseph and Joe.

NOVEMBER

At the Full Frosty Moon in November
I was in Englewood, interviewed by
David Evartic about Woody Allen and
I argued with Joseph about watching
television.

DECEMBER

At the Full Long Night Moon in December
I was having a difficult time at Englewood
imagining I could get out of the Actors
Home, where only Joseph comes to visit
me and some nights drives me to NYC.

2014

JANUARY

At the Cold Full Moon in January Tom comes early
in the day to proofread and correct *The Moon Poem*
which Dennis has typed up. Joseph comes to take
me to on a drive through Brooklyn which he loves
and calls his motherland.

FEBRUARY

At the Full Snow Moon in February it was St.
Valentine's Day, which I used to celebrate with
Julian, though we hardly celebrated any other
day. A huge snowstorm kept spirits down, and
guests away.

MARCH

At the Full Moon in March Garrick took me
to New York to watch Theodora Skipitares'
rehearsal of Ionesco's *The Chairs*. His chaperone
I pretend to be.

APRIL

At the Full Moon in April I still lived in the Actors
Home in Englewood, NJ and am not happy here.

MAY

At the Full Moon in May I was put downstairs in the nursing home to my great distress, for what they call Rehab.

JUNE

At the Full Moon in June I was still in the nursing home though they kept promising me to return me to my room. I watch the news about the brink of war between Israel and Palestine, and the thousands of children who are endangering their lives trying to find a better life.

JULY

At the Full Moon in July all my friends are trying to get me out of the nursing home where I've been all told I can never go back to my old room, and where I can't telephone, and can't go out into the garden.

After July 2014, Judith Malina did not always continue her Full Moon entries; writing became difficult. However, on the Full Moon in April of 2015 she celebrated the Seder at Lillian Booth with Garrick, Tom, Brad, Leah, Ilion, Karen and George, Lois and Charles, Cindy, and Gaia. She passed away five days later on April 10th at the age of 88.

The Living Theatre she co-founded with Julian Beck continues.

ABOUT JUDITH MALINA

Judith Malina trained with Erwin Piscator at the New School for Social Research in New York, where the pioneering director established a "Dramatic Workshop" during his exile from Nazi Germany in the mid-1940's.

In 1947 she and painter Julian Beck founded The Living Theatre as an artistic and socially-conscious alternative to the commercial theater. Since then she directed (and often acted in) more than sixty important productions which have had considerable influence on the development of contemporary theater, including William Carlos Williams' *Many Loves*, Jack Gelber's *The Connection*, Kenneth H. Brown's *The Brig*, Bertolt Brecht's *Antigone* and the collective creations *Mysteries and Smaller Pieces, Frankenstein, Paradise Now,* and *The Legacy of Cain.*

Judith Malina, along with The Living Theatre Company, was arrested and imprisoned in various countries for the theatrical expression of the group's anarchist-pacifist principle. Following the untimely death of Julian Beck in 1985, she directed the company alongside Hanon Reznikov, whom she married in 1988.

Malina was the author of numerous published essays on theatre and politics, diaries, poems and plays, and occasionally appeared as an actress in films (*Dog Day Afternoon, China Girl, Awakenings, Enemies: A Love Story, The Addams Family, Household Saints,* and *When in Rome.* She has taught at Columbia University, New York University, and the New School for Social Research. She was a 1996 recipient of an Honorary Doctorate from Whittier College.

In 1989, The Living Theatre opened a New York City performance space in the East Village at Third Street and Avenue C, which was active until the early nineties.

In 1999, she and Hanon Reznikov opened the Centro Living Europa, the European headquarters of The Living Theatre in the Palazzo Spinola of Rocchetta Ligure, Italy.

In 2007, The Living Theatre established a performance space in the Lower East Side of New York City, which served as its home until it was evicted in 2013. In 2014, the troupe staged Malina's *Nowhere to Hide* at the Burning Man Festival.

In 1975, Malina was given a lifetime achievement Obie award; she was a recipient of a 1985 Guggenheim award; in 2003, she was inducted into the Theatre Hall of Fame; and in 2008, she was awarded the Brazilian President's Medal for Outstanding Artistic Achievement.

On April 10, 2015, Malina died at the Lillian Booth Actors Home in Englewood, New Jersey at the age of eighty-eight. The Living Theatre continues to perform around the world.

RECENT AND FORTHCOMING BOOKS FROM THREE ROOMS PRESS

FICTION

Meagan Brothers
Weird Girl and What's His Name

Ron Dakron
Hello Devilfish!

Michael T. Fournier
Hidden Wheel
Swing State

Janet Hamill
Tales from the Eternal Café
(Introduction by Patti Smith)

Eamon Loingsigh
Light of the Diddicoy
Exile on Bridge Street

Aram Saroyan
Still Night in L.A.

Richard Vetere
The Writers Afterlife
Champagne and Cocaine

MEMOIR & BIOGRAPHY

Nassrine Azimi and
Michel Wasserman
Last Boat to Yokohama:
The Life and Legacy of
Beate Sirota Gordon

James Carr
BAD: The Autobiography of
James Carr

Richard Katrovas
Raising Girls in Bohemia:
Meditations of an American Father;
A Memoir in Essays

Judith Malina
Full Moon Stages: Personal Notes
from 50 Years of The Living Theatre

Stephen Spotte
My Watery Self:
Memoirs of a Marine Scientist

HUMOR

Peter Carlaftes
A Year on Facebook

PHOTOGRAPHY-MEMOIR

Mike Watt
On & Off Bass

SHORT STORY ANTHOLOGY

Dark City Lights: New York Stories
edited by Lawrence Block

Have a NYC I, II & III:
New York Short Stories;
edited by Peter Carlaftes
& Kat Georges

Quarter-Life Crisis:
An Anthology of Millenial Writers
edited by Constance Renfrow

This Way to End Times:
Classic and New Stories of
the Apocalypse
edited by Robert Silverberg

MIXED MEDIA

John S. Paul
Sign Language: A Painter's
Notebook (photography, poetry
and prose)

TRANSLATIONS

Thomas Bernhard
On Earth and in Hell
(poems of Thomas Bernhard
with English translations by
Peter Waugh)

Patrizia Gattaceca
Isula d'Anima / Soul Island
(poems by the author
in Corsican with English
translations)

César Vallejo | Gerard Malanga
Malanga Chasing Vallejo
(selected poems of César Vallejo
with English translations
and additional notes by
Gerard Malanga)

George Wallace
EOS: Abductor of Men
(selected poems of George
Wallace with Greek translations)

DADA

Maintenant: A Journal of
Contemporary Dada Writing & Art
(Annual, since 2008)

FILM & PLAYS

Israel Horovitz
My Old Lady: Complete Stage Play
and Screenplay with an Essay on
Adaptation

Peter Carlaftes
Triumph For Rent (3 Plays)
Teatrophy (3 More Plays)

POETRY COLLECTIONS

Hala Alyan
Atrium

Peter Carlaftes
DrunkYard Dog
I Fold with the Hand I Was Dealt

Thomas Fucaloro
It Starts from the Belly and Blooms
Inheriting Craziness is Like
a Soft Halo of Light

Kat Georges
Our Lady of the Hunger

Robert Gibbons
Close to the Tree

Israel Horovitz
Heaven and Other Poems

David Lawton
Sharp Blue Stream

Jane LeCroy
Signature Play

Philip Meersman
This is Belgian Chocolate

Jane Ormerod
Recreational Vehicles on Fire
Welcome to the Museum of Cattle

Lisa Panepinto
On This Borrowed Bike

George Wallace
Poppin' Johnny

Three Rooms Press | New York, NY | Current Catalog: www.threeroomspress.com
Three Rooms Press books are distributed by PGW/Perseus: www.pgw.com